What to Do With Your Life When You're 40 and Still Unsure

14 Unconventional Lessons

Jake Morimoto

Table of Contents

Author's Note	2
Download for FREE: 60 Questions That Will Make You Instantly Smarter (+ a special bonus)	3
Introduction: You're Not Late—You're Just Not Lying	7
1 - The Success You Wanted Then Might Be the Trap Now	14
2 - You're Not Behind. You're Just on Your Own Clock	23
3 - Midlife Isn't a Crisis: It's a Filter	34
4 - Small Experiments > Big Life Changes	46
5 - Stop Asking "What's My Purpose?"	57
6 - Quit Faster	69
7 - Your Job Isn't Who You Are (Anymore)	82
8 - There's No Medal for Exhaustion	93
9 - You Can Be Bad at It and Still Love It	104
10 - Be Useful, Not Impressive	117
11 - The Path Doesn't Have to Make Sense to Anyone But You	126
12 - You Can Be Both Grateful and Still Want More	136
13 - The Best Version of You Might Still Be in Beta	147
14 - The Point Isn't to Find What to Do With Your Life. It's to Live It	160
Conclusion: This Is Not the End of Something. It's a Middle Worth Loving.	170
A Tiny Favor That Would Mean the World to Me	178
My Other Books	179
Acknowledgments	182
About Jake	183
Bibliography	184

Copyright © 2025 by Jake Morimoto

All rights reserved. No part of this publication may be reproduced, distributed, or transmitted in any form or by any means, including photocopying, recording, or other electronic or mechanical methods, without the prior written permission of the publisher, except in the case of brief quotations embodied in critical reviews and certain other noncommercial uses permitted by copyright law.

ISBN: 979-8-9857158-5-9

For permission requests, contact hello@self-improvement.me

Published by Jake Morimoto

First Edition, 2025

Author's Note

This book is a collection of essays that forms part of the *Unconventional Wisdom* series.

You may notice that some essays draw on similar research or references. This is because they were originally written at different times as standalone pieces. When compiling this collection, I chose to preserve their original form for two reasons: first, the repetition reinforces key concepts central to the series; second, it allows readers the flexibility to dip into individual essays without needing to read the book cover to cover.

Whether you choose to read every essay or just a few, I hope you find something that resonates. Thank you for joining me on this journey, and I hope you enjoy the exploration.

JM

Download for FREE: 60 Questions That Will Make You Instantly Smarter (+ a special bonus)

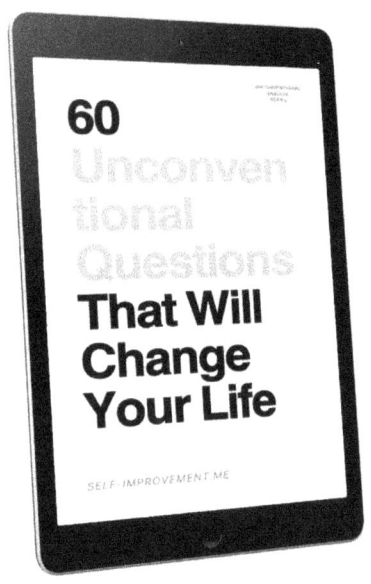

Unlock a **FREE** exclusive **60 Unconventional Questions That Will Change Your Life** from the *Unconventional Wisdom* series!

What if the right question could unlock a better version of you?

This free, short book is packed with *60 sharp, surprising, and thought-provoking questions* designed to challenge how you think, spark powerful reflection, and change the way you see yourself and the world.

These aren't your typical self-help prompts; they're unconventional, provocative, and designed to make you smarter, clearer, and more future-ready.

Inside, you'll explore:

- Questions to Spark Deep Reflection
- Questions to Challenge Perspectives
- Questions to Uncover Hidden Knowledge
- Questions to Sharpen Thinking & Decision-Making
- Questions to Predict the Future Better
- Questions to Expand Your Perspective
- Questions to Become Smarter Through Others
- Questions to Deepen Relationships

Plus, as a bonus, you'll also get **free access** to the *Introduction* and *First Chapter* of my book:

How To Be Respected: 14 Unconventional Lessons on How You Earn Respect—and Keep It: an unfiltered, smart guide to earning lasting respect in a noisy, distracted world.

Get it now. It's free—and it might just change the way you think forever.

Just scan the QR code below (or go to <u>self-improvement.me/wh</u>) and get them now:

Introduction: You're Not Late —You're Just Not Lying

The most persistent lie of adulthood is that everyone else has figured it out.

Look around at your next dinner party, workplace meeting, or school pickup line. Behind the confident nods and assured statements about five-year plans, most people are improvising their way through existence with the same questions that keep you up at night. The difference isn't that they've found answers. It's that they've gotten comfortable pretending they have.

At forty, you've reached a curious threshold—old enough to see through the performance, young enough to change course. This peculiar intersection of wisdom and possibility doesn't represent failure. It represents the first moment in your life when you might actually be ready to tell yourself the truth.

The truth is messy. It whispers that perhaps you've been chasing someone else's definition of success. It suggests that certainty might be overrated. It dares to ask whether the path you've been following has your footprints on it, or just the imprints of expectations you've inherited.

Most of our culture treats midlife questioning as a crisis—an embarrassing breakdown of certainty that should be quickly resolved and never mentioned again. We're supposed to have it all figured out by thirty, executing flawlessly by forty. The narrative goes something like this: early twenties for exploration, late twenties for commitment, thirties for advancement, forties for peak achievement. By midlife, you should be harvesting the fruits of decisions made when you were practically still adolescent.

What a peculiar expectation.

The novelist George Eliot once observed, "It is never too late to be what you might have been." But I would go further: it's never too late to discover who you actually are. And forty isn't late—it might be right on time.

Carl Jung, the Swiss psychiatrist whose work on personal development still resonates a century later, spoke of life as having two halves. The first half, roughly until midlife, involves establishing yourself in the world—career, family, social position. The second half is about meaning, integration, and individuation. Jung believed most people make the mistake of carrying the goals and strategies of life's first half into its second half, where they no longer serve.

In other words, what got you here won't get you there.

The pressure to have life "figured out" by forty stems from a fundamental misunderstanding of human development. We are not finished products by midlife; we are works in progress until our final breath. Psychologist Laura Carstensen at Stanford University has found through her research that emotional intelligence actually increases with age, alongside our ability to regulate emotions and prioritize meaningful experiences. The neuroplasticity of our brains—their ability to form new connections and pathways—continues throughout life. We remain capable of profound change, adaptation, and discovery at forty, fifty, sixty, and beyond.

Perhaps you've felt the subtle shame of not having arrived at some imaginary destination by now. A voice that says everyone else is content with their choices, fulfilled in their purpose, secure in their identity. Let me offer an alternative interpretation: you're not behind. You're just awake.

David Epstein, in his groundbreaking book "Range," chronicles how some of the world's most successful people take longer, more circuitous routes to finding their ultimate contribution. He challenges the "10,000 hours of deliberate practice" narrative by demonstrating how breadth of experience—sometimes appearing as indecision or career meandering—often leads to more innovative, satisfying work. The person who has tried many paths brings a richer perspective to whatever they ultimately do.

Remember filmmaker Ava DuVernay? She didn't pick up a camera until age 32, after a successful career in publicity. Her "late" entry into filmmaking didn't hinder her—it informed her unique perspective and approach. By 45, she had become the first Black female director to helm a $100 million film.

The intimidating thing about forty isn't the number. It's the growing suspicion that you can no longer blame circumstances, timing, or other people for the gap between the life you have and the life you want. It's the dawning realization that if something is going to change, you'll have to change it.

This realization isn't a crisis. It's an invitation.

Throughout my conversations with people navigating midlife transitions, I've noticed something striking: those who find their way through aren't necessarily the ones with the most resources, connections, or even clarity. They're the ones willing to question everything while still moving forward. They practice what investor Charlie Munger calls "worldly wisdom"—the ability to draw connections between disciplines and see patterns where others see chaos.

A former banking executive told me about the moment he realized he'd spent twenty years solving problems he didn't care about. "I wasn't failed by my career," he said. "I failed to notice I had outgrown it." At 44, he left to start a financial literacy program for teenagers in underserved communities. The work pays less but demands more of him—his creativity, his empathy, his full presence. "For the first time," he said, "I'm not just using my skills. I'm using myself."

His story illustrates a crucial point: confusion at forty doesn't mean you've done something wrong. It might mean you've done something right—you've remained honest enough with yourself to notice when the life you've built no longer fits the person you've become.

The essays that follow aren't about dramatic reinvention or finding the "perfect" answer to the question of what to do with your life. They're about something more fundamental: learning to ask better questions. Questions that cut through cultural conditioning about success, purpose, and fulfillment. Questions that honor the complexity of a human life at midpoint. Questions that create space for possibility rather than collapse it into premature certainty.

These questions matter because by forty, you've lived long enough to know that genuine fulfillment rarely comes from external markers. The promotion, the bigger house, the impressive title—these things shimmer with promise until they're achieved, then quickly become the new normal. Psychologists call this the "hedonic treadmill"—our tendency to quickly return to a relatively stable level of happiness despite major positive or negative events.

So if external achievements won't sustain us, what will? The research points consistently toward a few factors: meaningful work, deep relationships, autonomy, mastery, contribution to others, and alignment between our values and our daily lives. Notice that none of these require a particular career path, income level, or social status. They're available through countless configurations of life choices.

The psychologist Marsha Linehan observes that "the path to wisdom lies in the ability to hold opposing truths at once." At forty, you've earned the right to embrace contradiction: You can be both proud of what you've built and ready to tear it down. You can honor your past choices while making different ones now. You can acknowledge your limitations while expanding your possibilities.

A former client—a successful architect who felt increasingly alienated from her work—described her midlife questioning this way: "It's like I've been speaking a language fluently for twenty years, only to realize it's not my native tongue." At 47, she scaled back her practice to pursue a degree in environmental science. "People thought I was having a breakdown," she laughed. "But actually, I was having a breakthrough."

The essays ahead will challenge conventional wisdom about careers, purpose, identity, and what constitutes a well-lived life. They'll question the persistent American mythology that says we must constantly strive, achieve, and optimize. They'll suggest that perhaps the best parts of you are not the most productive or impressive parts. They'll propose that confusion might be a more honest response to life's complexity than certainty ever could be.

This book won't offer ten steps to clarity or promise that by the final page, you'll have a master plan for the rest of your days. Such promises would undermine the central argument here: that a meaningful life emerges not from having all the answers, but from asking better questions and staying awake to their unfolding answers.

What you'll find instead are invitations to think differently about this rich, complex season of life. To see your uncertainty not as a problem to solve but as perception finally clear enough to notice the cracks in simplistic narratives about success and fulfillment. To recognize that in a culture obsessed with knowing, there is radical power in admitting: "I'm still figuring it out."

Because the truth is, we all are. Some of us just stopped saying it out loud.

You're not late. You're not lost. You're just not lying anymore—not to yourself, not to others. And in that honesty, everything becomes possible again.

1 - The Success You Wanted Then Might Be the Trap Now

There's a peculiar alchemy that happens around age forty. The gold you once chased—that bright, shiny success you mapped out in your twenties—can suddenly feel like lead in your hands. Heavy. Constraining. Not at all what you thought it would be.

We don't talk about this enough. How the victory lap can feel like a prison yard. How the corner office with the view can become a gilded cage. How the success that consumed your youth might be the very thing suffocating you now.

This isn't about ingratitude. It's about honesty.

When I encounter people at midlife crossroads, the conversation almost always circles back to the same revelation: "I got what I wanted. And now I'm not sure I want it anymore." There's usually a pause after this confession, as if they've uttered something shameful. As if changing your mind about your life's direction is some sort of moral failing.

It isn't.

The dream job you landed at twenty-eight was chosen by a different version of you—someone with different values, different knowledge, and different priorities. You were making decisions with partial information, not just about the world, but about yourself. The psychological phenomenon known as the "end of history illusion" explains this perfectly. Coined by researchers Daniel Gilbert and Jordi Quoidbach, it describes our tendency to believe we've finished changing—that the person we are today is the person we'll be forever. Their studies showed that people consistently underestimate how much they'll change in the future, despite acknowledging how much they've changed in the past.

At twenty-five, you couldn't possibly know what forty would feel like. You were guessing, at best.

The story of Roger Horchow isn't widely known outside business circles, but it beautifully illustrates this turning point. Horchow built a luxury mail-order catalog empire that made him wealthy and respected. By conventional metrics, he'd "made it." Then at forty-something, he sold the company. Colleagues were baffled. Why walk away from such success? Because Horchow realized the business had become more about maintenance than meaning. He shifted to Broadway producing, helping create shows like "Crazy for You," finding a creative outlet that reawakened something in him. He didn't reject success—he redefined it.

The success you want at forty isn't always visual, measurable, or LinkedIn-friendly. It's often internal, textured, and impossible to capture in a résumé bullet point.

We cling to old definitions of success like life rafts, even when they're sinking us. The lawyer who hates practicing law but can't let go of the prestige. The executive who fantasizes about teaching but won't surrender the status.

The doctor who dreams of writing novels but can't abandon the identity she's spent decades building. The trap isn't the career itself—it's the death grip on a declining dream.

Harvard psychologist Daniel Gilbert's research on "affective forecasting" adds another layer to this dilemma. His studies demonstrate that humans are remarkably poor at predicting what will make them happy in the future. We consistently misjudge how long and intensely we'll feel emotions in response to both good and bad events. The promotion you once believed would bring lasting fulfillment likely delivered a shorter happiness boost than you anticipated. The failures you feared would devastate you probably didn't crush you for as long as you expected.

This isn't just academic theory—it's the explanation for that nagging sense of "is this it?" that haunts many successful forty-somethings.

A few years ago, I encountered a woman at a conference—let's call her Elaine. At forty-three, she had the legal career she'd plotted since high school: partner at a prestigious firm, respected in her field, financially secure. She also had a secret: she was profoundly unhappy. What began as private journaling about her dissatisfaction eventually led her to take a three-month sabbatical to work with a wildlife conservation project. Against every practical consideration, this corporate attorney found herself tracking endangered species through remote forests.

"I thought I was having a breakdown," she told me over coffee. "Then I realized I was having a breakthrough."

16

Elaine never returned to legal practice. She now works as a legal advisor for environmental organizations—making less money but feeling engaged in a way she hadn't for decades. The success she had achieved wasn't wrong; it just wasn't right anymore.

This pattern repeats endlessly across professions and personalities. The architect who realizes she wants to teach elementary school. The finance professional who dreams of running a small farm. The marketing executive who longs to become a therapist. These aren't failures of commitment or character. They're evidence of growth.

At forty, you're experiencing what psychologist Carol Gilligan might call an "integration crisis"—a necessary disruption where competing parts of yourself demand reconciliation. The ambitious competitor meets the person who craves meaning. The security-seeker confronts the risk-taker. The professional identity collides with other aspects of selfhood that have been lying dormant.

The trap tightens when we interpret these conflicts as weakness rather than wisdom.

Most self-help narratives around midlife focus on "finding your passion" or "reinventing yourself," as if you need to discard everything and start from zero. This misses the point. The challenge isn't to erase your past or reject your achievements. It's to recognize that the success template you've been following may have reached its expiration date.

Psychologist James Hollis speaks of the "second adulthood" that begins in midlife—a phase where the governing question shifts from "What does the world want from me?" to "What does the soul want from me?" This isn't mystical jargon. It's about moving from external validation to internal alignment.

The success that once motivated you likely came with scripts: If I achieve X, I'll be respected. If I earn Y, I'll be secure. If I reach position Z, I'll be fulfilled. These equations seemed reliable in your twenties and thirties. By forty, you've run the calculations enough times to know they don't always balance.

This realization can feel like failure. It's not. It's clarity.

A lesser-known study from the Harvard Business Review found that professionals who make significant career shifts in their forties often report higher satisfaction than those who stay on linear paths—not despite the disruption, but because of it. The research suggested that it wasn't the specific new direction that mattered most, but the act of choosing consciously rather than continuing through momentum.

Former NFL player John Urschel offers a compelling illustration of letting go of a successful path that no longer fits. As a Baltimore Ravens offensive lineman, Urschel achieved what countless young athletes dream of. Yet at twenty-six, he walked away from football at the height of his career to pursue mathematics. While technically younger than forty, his story captures the essence of recognizing when continued success in one arena might constrain your growth in another.

18

"I no longer wish to risk my health for a game," Urschel explained when he retired. But the deeper motivation was positive, not negative. His passion for mathematical research had grown to the point where football—despite its prestige and financial rewards—felt like a distraction from what truly engaged him.

Today, Urschel is completing a PhD in mathematics at MIT. The success he wanted then became the trap he needed to escape.

This isn't just about career. Success traps appear in every domain. The marriage that once felt like an achievement but now feels like an arrangement. The social circle that once validated you but now constrains you. The lifestyle that impressed others but never quite satisfied you.

At forty, these dissonances become harder to ignore.

What makes these transitions so challenging isn't necessarily the practical considerations, though those are real. It's the identity crisis that accompanies them. After decades of introducing yourself as a lawyer, doctor, executive, or expert, who are you if you step away from that role? When you've built a life around certain metrics of success, what happens when you change the measurements?

The writer David Foster Wallace captured this predicament perfectly: "The really important kind of freedom involves attention, and awareness, and discipline, and effort, and being able truly to care about other people and to sacrifice for them, over and over, in myriad petty little unsexy ways, every day." The freedom to redefine success at forty isn't about abandoning responsibility—it's about recommitting to what genuinely matters.

Sometimes the trap isn't even of your own making. Cultural narratives about "having it all" or "living your best life" create impossible standards that turn even objective successes into perceived failures. Social media amplifies this, presenting curated versions of others' lives against which you measure your messy reality.

By forty, you're experienced enough to see through these illusions, but that doesn't automatically free you from their influence.

Breaking free requires something counterintuitive: gratitude for the very success that now constrains you. That career provided security, skills, and experiences that make your current awareness possible. That relationship taught you about love, even if it's ending. That achievement opened doors, even if you're now walking through different ones.

The success wasn't wrong. It just served its purpose.

There's a wonderful concept in ecology called "succession"—how ecosystems naturally evolve through different stages, each one necessary for the next to emerge. What worked perfectly in one phase becomes limiting in another. The pioneering species that thrive after a forest fire create conditions that eventually make way for different plants. Nothing has failed; everything has served.

Your earlier success is like those pioneer species. It created conditions for something new to grow.

At forty, you have resources your younger self lacked: perspective, financial stability (maybe), self-knowledge, professional skills, and networks. The success that now feels constraining has given you tools to build something different.

What would happen if you saw your current dissatisfaction not as a midlife crisis but as midlife clarity? Not as failure but as graduation?

The trap loosens when you recognize that succeeding at something doesn't obligate you to do it forever. The trap breaks when you realize that changing direction isn't betrayal—it's growth.

There's a remarkable liberation in acknowledging that the success you wanted then might be the trap now. It creates space to ask better questions: What would success look like if I defined it today, from scratch? What felt like success when I wasn't looking? What kinds of accomplishment give me energy rather than depleting it?

The answers might surprise you. They might lead to dramatic external changes, or they might transform how you experience your existing life. They might redefine success entirely.

At forty, you don't need a new five-year plan. You need permission to question the plans that brought you here. You need the courage to acknowledge when yesterday's definition of success has become today's constraint.

The path forward isn't about abandonment. It's about integration. How can the skills, resources, and wisdom from your first-act success serve what calls to you now? How can you honor what was while creating what could be?

There's no universal playbook for this transition. Some people make radical external changes: new careers, relationships, locations. Others transform from within, bringing fresh energy and perspective to existing circumstances. The common thread isn't what changes, but the willingness to question yesterday's success template.

The success you wanted then might be the trap now. But here's the beautiful paradox: recognizing the trap is itself a form of success—perhaps the most meaningful kind. It means you're awake enough to notice the dissonance, brave enough to acknowledge it, and alive enough to do something about it.

That's not a midlife crisis. That's midlife courage.

2 - You're Not Behind. You're Just on Your Own Clock

Time has a funny way of becoming both enemy and obsession around age forty. The invisible stopwatch that's been silently tracking your progress since childhood suddenly seems to tick more loudly. The quiet whisper of "by now, I should have..." grows into a persistent roar. The milestones you once anticipated—career peaks, relationship landmarks, financial targets—seem to be flying past your window while you're still fumbling with the map.

But what if you're not actually behind? What if you're simply operating on your own clock?

The modern world runs on standardized time. Our lives are measured in quarters, fiscal years, five-year plans, and decades. We're expected to follow predictable trajectories: education by your twenties, career establishment by your thirties, peak achievement by your forties, and graceful descent thereafter. This collective fiction about timing is so pervasive that we rarely question it. Like fish unaware of water, we swim through these temporal expectations without noticing how arbitrary they actually are.

The tyranny of timelines begins early. Remember the first time someone asked what you wanted to be when you grew up? You were probably still learning to tie your shoes, yet adults expected you to have mapped out your professional destiny. By high school, guidance counselors wanted five-year plans. By college, interviewers asked about ten-year goals. The cultural message was clear: life is a race with fixed checkpoints, and the winners reach them on schedule.

By forty, we've internalized these artificial timelines so deeply that deviating from them feels like failure. But here's the liberating truth: these societal clocks have nothing to do with your actual development, potential, or path to fulfillment. They're convenient fictions, not biological laws.

The story of NFL quarterback Kurt Warner offers a stunning rebuke to our obsession with "correct" timing. Unlike the standard professional athlete narrative of early recognition and meteoric rise, Warner's path was wildly nonlinear. After going undrafted out of college, he was cut by the Green Bay Packers and found himself stocking shelves at an Iowa grocery store for $5.50 an hour. At twenty-seven—an age when most professional footballers are hitting their stride—Warner was bagging groceries and playing for the Iowa Barnstormers in the Arena Football League.

Most sports narratives would end there. The window had closed. The timing was wrong. The opportunity had passed.

But Warner's biological clock didn't sync with football's expectations. At twenty-eight, he signed with the St. Louis Rams as a backup quarterback. When the starting quarterback suffered a preseason injury, Warner stepped in and delivered one of the most remarkable seasons in NFL history. He won the league MVP award, led the Rams to a Super Bowl victory, and was named Super Bowl MVP—all within eighteen months of stocking shelves at a supermarket.

Warner didn't suddenly develop talent at twenty-eight. He had always been capable. The world's timeline simply hadn't aligned with his development until that moment. Had he internalized society's message that athletes peak in their early twenties, he might have abandoned his dream and never discovered what was possible.

This pattern repeats across domains. Fashion designer Vera Wang didn't start designing clothes until she was forty, after a career as a figure skater and fashion editor. Stan Lee created the Fantastic Four at thirty-nine and Spider-Man at forty, revolutionizing comic books after nearly two decades of unremarkable work in the industry. Raymond Chandler published his first novel at fifty-one. Martha Stewart built her empire after forty. Morgan Freeman became a household name in his fifties.

The "late bloomer" narrative might seem comforting, but it actually reinforces the problem. The very term "late bloomer" accepts the premise that there's a "right time" to bloom. It subtly suggests that developing on your own schedule is an exception, not the rule. It pathologizes normal human variation.

A less-known but fascinating study from the University of Pennsylvania examined career trajectories across multiple fields and found something surprising: there is no single pattern of creative or professional development. Some people are indeed "early bloomers" who make their mark young. Others are "late bloomers" who hit their stride at advanced ages. Still others show a steady, gradual climb throughout life, while some experience multiple peaks and valleys.

The researchers identified what they called "dark horses"—professionals whose success came through unconventional timing and unexpected routes. These individuals typically shared one characteristic: they ignored standard timelines and instead focused on finding the right fit between their evolving capabilities and the right opportunities.

The mythology of correct timing doesn't just distort our professional lives—it warps our personal development as well. We've created arbitrary markers for when people should partner up, have children, buy homes, or find their "passion." Miss these windows, and society implies you've somehow failed at the basic business of living.

A particularly pernicious timeline myth involves creativity and innovation. We've romanticized youth as the wellspring of originality, enshrining the image of the twenty-something genius changing the world from a garage. Yet the data tells a different story. A comprehensive study of Nobel Prize winners found that the average age of laureates has increased significantly over the past century. The researchers discovered that major creative and scientific breakthroughs now typically come from individuals in their forties, fifties, and beyond.

The same pattern appears in entrepreneurship, despite Silicon Valley's youth obsession. The average age of successful startup founders is approximately forty-five. The mythology of the wunderkind obscures the reality that innovation often requires the patience, perspective, and resilience that come with time.

Time operates differently for each of us. While chronological time marches forward at the same rate for everyone, psychological time—our internal experience of duration, development, and readiness—varies wildly between individuals. What takes one person five years to process might require another person fifteen. What one person is prepared to attempt at thirty, another might not be ready for until fifty.

This variance isn't weakness or inefficiency—it's human nature. Our developmental timelines are as unique as our fingerprints, shaped by temperament, circumstance, early experiences, and countless invisible factors. Yet we insist on measuring everyone against the same arbitrary clock.

The author Malcolm Gladwell explored this phenomenon in his lesser-known essay "Late Bloomers," where he contrasts Picasso's early brilliance with Cézanne's gradual development. Picasso produced masterpieces in his twenties, while Cézanne's greatest works came after decades of experimentation. Neither timeline was "correct"—they simply reflected different creative processes. Cézanne wasn't behind; he was on his own clock.

What makes this timing anxiety particularly acute at forty is the growing awareness of mortality. The midpoint of life (give or take) naturally prompts reflection on what remains undone. But this existential math problem becomes unnecessarily painful when filtered through society's expectations about correct timing.

Perhaps no writer captured this better than George Eliot in her novel "Middlemarch," where she wrote of her character Dorothea: "Her full nature spent itself in channels which had no great name on the earth. But the effect of her being on those around her was incalculably diffusive: for the growing good of the world is partly dependent on unhistoric acts." Eliot was suggesting that meaningful life often unfolds outside the timelines of public recognition or achievement.

The question changes at forty. Instead of "Am I on schedule?" the better question becomes "Whose schedule am I on?" Instead of "Am I behind?" ask "Behind according to whom?"

The most insidious aspect of timeline tyranny is how it steals present joy by creating artificial anxiety about the future. When you believe you're behind, you live in a perpetual state of catching up. The present moment becomes merely a means to reach some imagined future where you'll finally be "on track." But that future rarely arrives, because the same timeline mentality will create new standards you haven't yet met.

This isn't an argument for complacency or against ambition. It's a call to reclaim your own developmental rhythm—to recognize that growth doesn't conform to quarterly reports or five-year plans. Some seasons are for rapid expansion, others for consolidation, still others for fallow periods that prepare the soil for later blooming.

In physics, Einstein's theory of relativity demonstrated that time itself is not absolute but relative to the observer's position and movement. Similarly, your life's timing is relative to your unique position and journey—not to some universal standard of correct development.

The pioneering psychologist Carl Rogers observed that human development isn't linear but spiral-shaped, with themes and challenges recurring at different levels throughout life. We don't simply progress from point A to point B; we revisit similar questions with greater depth and nuance as we age. This spiral model better reflects how humans actually grow than does our cultural straight-line narrative.

Researchers studying developmental psychology have identified what they call "non-normative life transitions"— changes that occur off the expected timeline or in unexpected order. These transitions were once considered problematic deviations. More recent research reveals that these non-normative patterns often lead to greater resilience and adaptability. Put simply: following an unconventional timeline might actually make you stronger, not weaker.

At forty, this perspective offers liberation from the fear of being "behind." If development is spiral rather than linear, if timing is relative rather than absolute, if growth follows unique patterns rather than standardized trajectories— then the very concept of "behind" loses its meaning.

A less discussed but equally important dimension involves emotional and psychological development. Some people develop emotional intelligence early. Others come to it gradually through life experience. Some find their values clarified in youth, while others require decades of experimentation to discover what truly matters to them. Neither timeline is superior; they're simply different paths to wisdom.

The Norwegian chess grandmaster Simen Agdestein offers an unusual example of personal timing. He pursued professional soccer and chess simultaneously, representing Norway's national team in soccer while competing as a chess grandmaster. Each field has its own expected timeline of development, yet Agdestein refused to choose between them or to follow either field's standard trajectory. Instead, he created his own developmental schedule, becoming the only person to compete at international levels in both pursuits.

Timing isn't just about when things happen—it's about the sequence in which they unfold. The order of your life experiences shapes how you interpret and integrate them. Someone who finds career success before starting a family will process that experience differently than someone who starts a family first. Neither sequence is inherently better; they simply create different perspectives.

This sequencing effect explains why certain insights or opportunities arrive when they do. The forty-year-old who suddenly feels drawn to a new field isn't experiencing a random impulse. They're responding to the unique constellation of experiences, skills, and wisdom they've accumulated in a particular order. Their timing is perfect—not according to society's clock, but according to their own developmental sequence.

When we force artificial timelines onto this natural sequencing, we interrupt the organic unfolding of potential. It's like demanding that a rose bloom in winter because that's when you scheduled the garden party. The rose isn't late; the party is simply misaligned with the flower's natural cycle.

The most common regret expressed by the dying, according to palliative care workers, isn't about missed promotions or unachieved status. It's about living according to others' expectations rather than one's own truth. At forty, you still have time to correct this mistake—to align your remaining decades with your actual values and rhythm rather than with inherited timelines.

What might change if you embraced your own clock? You might give yourself permission to be a beginner at forty-something. You might recognize that your current dissatisfaction isn't a failure but a necessary stage in your unique spiral of growth. You might see that your timing hasn't been wrong—it's been yours.

The ancient Greeks distinguished between two types of time: chronos (sequential, measurable time) and kairos (the right or opportune moment). While we can't control chronos—the march of days and years—we can develop sensitivity to kairos—the moments that are ripe for particular actions or changes. At forty, the question shifts from "Am I on time?" to "Is this the right time for me?"

Those who thrive in their forties, fifties, and beyond aren't those who most closely adhered to standard timelines. They're those who learned to read their own seasons, who recognized when to push forward and when to lie fallow, who understood that development has its own intelligence that doesn't conform to external schedules.

What would happen if you stopped checking your progress against arbitrary markers and instead asked: What is my system trying to tell me about my own timing? What is trying to emerge now, regardless of whether it's "on schedule"? What if my perceived delays aren't delays at all, but necessary incubation periods?

Perhaps you aren't behind. Perhaps you've been exactly where you needed to be all along, gathering experiences and insights that will prove essential for what comes next. Perhaps your timing hasn't been wrong—just different. And perhaps that difference is precisely what the world needs from you.

The cultural pressure to follow standardized timelines doesn't just create unnecessary anxiety—it actively reduces human potential. When we force ourselves to develop on artificial schedules, we cut short the natural incubation periods that lead to our most meaningful contributions. We harvest the fruit before it's ripe.

At forty, you have a choice. You can continue measuring yourself against arbitrary timelines that were never designed for your unique path. Or you can reclaim your own developmental rhythm—recognizing that you aren't behind; you're just on your own clock.

This isn't about lowering standards or abandoning ambition. It's about aligning your expectations with your actual development rather than with cultural fictions about timing. It's about trusting the intelligence of your own growth pattern, even when it doesn't match the standard trajectory.

Time isn't your enemy at forty. Artificial timelines are. The ticking clock that haunts you isn't measuring objective reality—it's measuring your adherence to collective myths about when things "should" happen.

You're not behind. You're not late. You're right on time for your life.

3 - Midlife Isn't a Crisis: It's a Filter

The phrase "midlife crisis" has become such a familiar cultural trope that we barely question its validity. We picture the stereotypical man in his forties purchasing a flashy red sports car or the woman suddenly quitting her stable job to backpack across Southeast Asia. These images are so deeply ingrained in our collective consciousness that when we reach our forties and begin questioning our life choices, we immediately wonder if we're experiencing this supposedly inevitable breakdown.

But what if we've been looking at midlife all wrong? What if this period of intense questioning isn't a crisis at all, but rather the first time many of us are finally honest enough with ourselves to see clearly?

Midlife isn't a crisis—it's a filter.

It's the moment when the accumulated wisdom of four decades suddenly crystallizes into a finely-tuned detection system that separates truth from performance, authentic desires from inherited expectations, and what actually matters from what merely impresses others. The discomfort so many experience at midlife isn't a malfunction—it's the system working exactly as it should.

The filter activates when you're finally old enough to tell the truth—to yourself, above all.

In your twenties and thirties, most of your energy goes toward establishing yourself: building credentials, proving competence, securing partnerships, creating stability. This phase requires a certain kind of performance, and often, a willingness to temporarily suppress parts of yourself that don't fit neatly into these projects. You accommodate, adapt, and sometimes acquiesce because you're still building the foundation.

By forty, the foundation is largely built. The pressing concerns of early adulthood—basic security, initial career advancement, family formation—have either been addressed or revealed themselves as irrelevant to your particular path. The volume on those urgent demands turns down just enough that you can finally hear a quieter voice that's been there all along, asking: "Is this really what you want? Does this actually matter? Are you becoming who you truly are, or merely what seemed sensible at twenty-five?"

This questioning isn't a breakdown of meaning—it's a breakthrough of authenticity.

Psychologist Elliot Jaques, who first coined the term "midlife crisis" in 1965, actually described something far more nuanced than today's caricature. Jaques observed that around age forty, many accomplished individuals experienced a profound shift in how they related to time, mortality, and meaning. It wasn't primarily about regret or desire for youth—it was about confronting the gap between the life they'd built and the person they actually were.

This gap exists for nearly everyone, but it's especially pronounced for those who've been highly successful by conventional standards. Success often requires conformity to external metrics and expectations. The more successful you've been at meeting those external standards, the more likely you've had to sideline certain authentic aspects of yourself along the way. The midlife filter simply makes this trade-off visible, often for the first time.

A lesser-known but fascinating study conducted by researchers at the University of Greenwich tracked professionals through midlife transitions. They found something surprising: those who experienced the most acute "crisis" symptoms were often those who had been most conventionally successful. The researchers concluded that the distress wasn't about failure, but about "success in the wrong direction"—achievement that led away from, rather than toward, the individual's core values and identity.

The discomfort that arises at midlife is your inner coherence detector activating. It's scanning for misalignment between your external life and your internal truth, between what you've achieved and who you actually are. And because almost no one reaches forty without some degree of compromise or conformity, the detector nearly always finds something.

The filter isn't just identifying what's false—it's clarifying what's true. Contrary to popular belief, midlife isn't primarily about what you're giving up or leaving behind. It's about what you're finally able to see and claim.

This clarification process often appears in unexpected domains. Take Katherine, a high-powered marketing executive who, after fifteen years of climbing the corporate ladder, suddenly found herself unable to generate enthusiasm for her work. The presentations that once energized her now felt hollow. The strategies that previously engaged her creativity now seemed like empty exercises.

Her initial response was panic: Was she burning out? Experiencing depression? Having a midlife crisis?

What Katherine discovered through careful self-examination was more subtle. Her distress wasn't about the work itself, but about the growing gap between the corporate narratives she was crafting and the actual impact of those products on consumers' lives. The marketing language she'd once used unquestioningly now triggered an internal alarm. Her "crisis" wasn't a breakdown—it was her integrity coming online with new strength.

Within a year, Katherine left her corporate role to establish a small consultancy focused exclusively on organizations with demonstrable social benefits. Her income dropped by half, her hours remained much the same, but the alignment between her work and her values eliminated the distress entirely. The filter had done its job.

This pattern repeats across countless lives. The filter doesn't always lead to dramatic external changes, but it invariably demands greater internal honesty. Sometimes the necessary adjustment is relatively minor—a shift in perspective or priority rather than profession. Other times, the misalignment is so fundamental that only a significant life renovation will resolve it.

Researchers at the Midlife in the United States (MIDUS) project have spent decades tracking thousands of Americans through midlife. Their findings contradict many popular assumptions about this phase. Far from being a universal period of crisis, they found that midlife is often characterized by increased psychological well-being for those who respond to its challenges by becoming more authentic rather than more conforming.

The filter's effectiveness depends on your willingness to trust what it reveals. Many people experience the initial discomfort—the restlessness, questioning, or dissatisfaction—but then immediately attempt to suppress these signals. They double down on external validation, accumulate more achievements, or distract themselves with consumption. This approach doesn't eliminate the filter's function; it merely postpones its revelations.

The midlife filter is particularly sensitive to three specific types of misalignment: values misalignment (when your actions contradict what matters most to you), identity misalignment (when your role conflicts with your authentic self), and vitality misalignment (when your lifestyle drains rather than sustains your energy). The discomfort emerges precisely because the filter is working—identifying exactly where these gaps exist.

What makes this filter especially powerful at midlife is the unique combination of experience and time. At forty,

38

you've lived long enough to recognize patterns, understand consequences, and discern what truly matters to you. Yet you likely have decades ahead—time enough to make meaningful changes based on these insights. This intersection of wisdom and opportunity is what makes midlife filtering so potent.

The story of Marion Stokes offers an extraordinary illustration of the midlife filter at work. Stokes spent the first half of her professional life as a librarian and television producer in Philadelphia. Around age forty-five, she began what many surely viewed as an eccentric obsession: recording television news broadcasts. For the next thirty-plus years, until her death at age eighty-three, Stokes continuously recorded television news on multiple channels, eventually amassing over 70,000 videotapes—the largest known collection of television news recorded by a single person.

What appeared to many as an unusual hobby was actually a profound act of cultural preservation. Stokes recognized something that major media archives and institutions missed: the ephemeral nature of broadcast news and its historical significance. Her midlife filter cut through conventional assumptions about what was worth preserving and revealed a genuine cultural need. Today, her collection is recognized as an invaluable historical archive, containing footage that would otherwise have been lost forever.

Stokes didn't experience a crisis—she experienced clarity about what mattered to her, regardless of whether others understood.

The midlife filter often reveals truths that have been hiding in plain sight. Take Emma, a corporate accountant who, at forty-two, left her well-paying position to run a rural animal sanctuary. To outside observers, this appeared to be a classic midlife crisis—abandoning security for a seemingly impulsive passion. But Emma's story was far more cohesive than it appeared.

Since childhood, Emma had felt a deep connection to animals and environmental causes. Throughout her education and early career, she had sidelined these interests as "impractical" while pursuing financial security. The accounting career wasn't a mistake—it provided skills and resources she would later need. But it was always a means, never an end. By her early forties, with financial stability established and core skills developed, the filter simply revealed what had always been true: her deepest satisfaction came from direct care of animals and land.

Emma didn't suddenly become a different person—she finally stopped pretending to be someone she wasn't. The filter didn't create new values; it merely stripped away the accumulated layers of accommodation and compromise that had obscured her longstanding ones.

This pattern of reclaiming suppressed aspects of the self appears repeatedly in midlife transitions. The executive who returns to the music he abandoned after college. The teacher who finally writes the novel she's been planning for decades. The engineer who acknowledges his desire to work with his hands rather than just his mind. These aren't new impulses—they're original ones that were temporarily set aside during the establishment phase of adulthood.

The midlife filter doesn't just clarify what matters—it also reveals what doesn't. This negative filtering function is equally valuable, though often less comfortable. It shows you where you've been performing rather than being, where you've been seeking approval rather than satisfaction, where you've been accumulating rather than experiencing.

Psychologist Abraham Maslow, best known for his hierarchy of needs, observed something intriguing about individuals who reached what he called "self-actualization." As people moved toward greater authenticity, they simultaneously became more discerning about how they spent their time and attention. They didn't just add new interests—they actively eliminated experiences, relationships, and activities that no longer aligned with their core values.

This process of elimination is a crucial function of the midlife filter. It's not just about discovering what truly matters to you—it's about creating the space for those priorities by filtering out what doesn't. This often requires saying no to opportunities that would have been automatic yeses in your thirties, declining invitations that once seemed essential, and sometimes disappointing people who expect you to remain unchanged.

The efficiency of this filtering process is what sometimes makes midlife appear abrupt or unsettling to outside observers. When someone spends years accumulating misalignments between their external life and internal values, the corrections, when they finally come, can seem sudden and dramatic. The executive who quits to start a bakery, the suburban parent who moves to a rural homestead, the professional who steps away from a prestigious career to care for family—these transitions appear extreme only because the previous misalignment was so profound.

The midlife filter also reveals something essential about the nature of adulthood itself: it's not a static state but an evolving process. The person you were at twenty-five needed different things than the person you are at forty-five. The challenges that engaged you then may bore you now. The sacrifices that made sense in one context may be pointless in another. This evolution isn't failure—it's maturation.

Cultural anthropologist Mary Catherine Bateson captured this developmental perspective beautifully in her concept of "composing a life." Rather than seeing adulthood as the implementation of a single, fixed plan, Bateson described it as an ongoing creative process of adaptation and integration. From this perspective, midlife recalibration isn't a crisis—it's a natural creative adjustment in a well-composed life.

The filter doesn't just operate on career or external achievement—it scrutinizes relationships with equal accuracy. Friendships that were based primarily on proximity or convenience rather than genuine connection often don't survive the filtering process. Romantic partnerships that were founded more on mutual goals than mutual understanding face new challenges. Family relationships based on obligation rather than authenticity become increasingly difficult to maintain without modification.

This relational filtering can be among the most painful aspects of midlife, but also the most liberating. The relationships that pass through the filter—those based on genuine connection, mutual growth, and shared values—often deepen substantially. Meanwhile, those that were primarily transactional or performative either transform or fade away.

The power of the midlife filter ultimately depends on whether you treat it as an ally or an enemy. Approached with resistance and fear, it becomes the dreaded "crisis" of popular imagination—a disruptive force that threatens stability and identity. Embraced as a natural developmental tool, it becomes a clarifying lens that reveals what's been true all along.

The discomfort that accompanies this filtering process isn't pathological—it's informational. It tells you exactly where attention is needed, where alignment is lacking, where truth has been compromised. The distress signals aren't the problem; they're the solution beginning to emerge.

This perspective transforms how we understand the common experiences of midlife: the restlessness, questioning, and reevaluation. Rather than symptoms of breakdown, they become evidence of breakthrough—signs that the system is working exactly as designed, filtering truth from performance, authenticity from accommodation, and meaning from mere success.

The filter activates around forty not because something has gone wrong, but because you're finally ready for a more authentic expression of who you are. You have enough experience to know what matters, enough security to risk change, enough perspective to see patterns, and—crucially—enough time remaining to act on these insights.

This framing transforms midlife from a period of crisis to one of opportunity. Instead of fearing the questions that arise, you can welcome them as guides toward greater alignment. Instead of resisting the discomfort, you can recognize it as the necessary friction that occurs when truth encounters compromise.

The midlife filter offers a remarkable gift: the chance to live the second half of your adult life with greater authenticity than the first. It reveals what you've always known but perhaps couldn't acknowledge. It clarifies what truly matters to you beneath the accumulated layers of should, must, and ought. It distinguishes between the life you've constructed and the life that would actually satisfy you.

This filter doesn't demand dramatic external changes, though those sometimes follow. What it requires is internal honesty—a willingness to see clearly what is and isn't working, what does and doesn't matter, what is and isn't truly yours. The external adjustments, when they come, are simply the natural expression of this greater clarity.

Midlife isn't asking you to blow up your life. It's asking you to see it accurately, perhaps for the first time. It's offering you the opportunity to filter out what isn't serving your authentic development and to focus your remaining decades on what genuinely matters to you.

This isn't a crisis. It's a clarification.

Your forties aren't a breakdown—they're a breakthrough of truth-telling, when you're finally old enough to know what matters and still young enough to act on that knowledge. The discomfort isn't the problem; it's the solution emerging. The filter isn't failing; it's finally working.

And that might be the most valuable midlife revelation of all.

4 - Small Experiments > Big Life Changes

There's a special kind of panic that arrives around midlife—a sense that if you haven't figured it all out by now, you'd better make some dramatic change, and fast. Society feeds us stories of radical reinvention: the banker who sold everything to open a vineyard, the executive who walked away from corporate life to live in Bali, the suburban parent who suddenly decides to become a minimalist nomad. We're enchanted by these tales because they promise a clean slate, a dramatic before-and-after that signals to ourselves and others that we've decisively addressed our discontent.

But what if the pressure to make sweeping life changes is actually the problem, not the solution?

The mythology of the midlife transformation follows a familiar script: you wake up one day, realize you've been living someone else's dream, dramatically quit your job, perhaps sell your possessions, and emerge like a butterfly from its chrysalis—fundamentally transformed. It's cinematic. It's inspiring. And for most of us, it's completely unrealistic.

Here's a truth that rarely makes for compelling movie plots: lasting change typically happens through small, incremental shifts rather than dramatic overhauls. The person who suddenly quits their job without a plan is more likely to face regret than revelation. The midlife career-changer who succeeds usually dips their toes in the water first, testing and learning before fully committing.

When you're 40 and uncertain, you don't need a new life. You need information—about yourself, about possibilities, about what actually energizes you rather than what you think should energize you. And the most reliable way to gather that information isn't through grand pronouncements or irreversible decisions. It's through small experiments.

The term "small experiments" might sound underwhelming when what you crave is transformation. But there's hidden power in this approach that the dramatic life-changers often miss. Small bets allow you to test reality without betting the farm. They create space for discovery without the pressure of immediate success. Most importantly, they honor the complexity of who you are at 40—someone with responsibilities, relationships, and resources you've spent decades building.

Richard Freeman was 42 when he began to question his two-decade career in marketing. The conventional midlife crisis playbook would have suggested dramatic action: quit, enroll in a completely different field, perhaps go back to school full-time. Instead, Freeman created what he calls a "learning lab" in his own life. He began taking a single community college course in structural engineering—a field that had always fascinated him. One evening a week, for sixteen weeks.

"I didn't tell my colleagues or even most of my friends," Freeman explained. "It wasn't about making a statement or even about definitely changing careers. It was just about putting myself in a new environment and seeing how it felt."

That single course didn't immediately transform Freeman's life. But it gave him crucial data: he discovered he loved the precision of engineering but dreaded the required mathematics. He liked being a student again, but not the heavy theoretical components. These insights led to his next small experiment: shadowing a friend who worked in architectural project management for a weekend.

Three small experiments and eight months later, Freeman hadn't dramatically "reinvented himself." Instead, he'd gathered enough information to make a lateral move within his existing company to a role that incorporated the elements of built environments he'd discovered he enjoyed, while utilizing the marketing expertise he'd developed over decades. The change wasn't cinematically satisfying to outsiders, but it addressed his actual dissatisfaction without requiring him to discard the equity he'd built over his career.

"The biggest surprise," Freeman reflects, "was realizing I didn't need to blow up my life to change it. I just needed to pay attention and make small adjustments based on what I was learning."

This approach—making small bets to gather information before committing to larger changes—borrows from a methodology that transformed product development in the tech world. Software developers discovered that building entire systems based on initial assumptions often led to spectacular failures. Instead, they adopted agile development: build something small, test it with real users, learn from the results, and iterate. The result has been products that actually meet user needs rather than what developers imagined those needs might be.

When applied to your midlife journey, this same logic is transformative. Rather than making life decisions based on untested assumptions about what might make you happy, you can run small experiments to gather actual data. The results are often surprising.

Author and entrepreneur Seth Godin articulates this approach in his book "The Dip," where he distinguishes between strategic quitting and impulsive quitting. The midlife urge is often to impulsively quit—to walk away from what isn't working without clarity about what comes next. Godin suggests instead a more nuanced approach: identifying the smallest viable test that could give you information about whether a new direction has potential.

Consider Marianne Kelly, who at 43 had spent two decades in corporate finance but harbored a long-standing interest in interior design. The conventional approach might have been to quit her job and start a design business, or go back to school full-time for formal training. Instead, Kelly created a 90-day challenge for herself: spend ten hours each weekend redesigning friends' spaces for free, documenting the before and after, and collecting honest feedback.

"I wasn't trying to prove I could make a living at it immediately," Kelly explains. "I was trying to answer basic questions: Did I actually enjoy the work when I was doing it regularly, not just occasionally? Was I any good at it? What parts of the process energized me versus drained me?"

Her small experiment yielded surprising results. While she loved the creative aspects of interior design, she discovered she didn't enjoy the client management components—the very thing that would be required to build a successful business. Rather than abandoning her finance career for a new profession that might not actually bring satisfaction, Kelly used this information to create a hybrid approach: she remained in finance but began specializing in real estate portfolios, where her developing aesthetic sensibilities gave her an edge, while pursuing design as a serious hobby rather than a business.

"If I had made the big jump without testing it first, I might have ended up just as dissatisfied but with the added stress of starting over financially," she notes. "Small experiments let me integrate what I learned about myself without having to throw away everything I'd built."

This approach challenges one of our most persistent cultural myths: that meaningful change requires dramatic action. We've been conditioned to believe that anything worth doing demands complete commitment—going "all in" is romanticized as the mark of serious intent. But this binary thinking—you're either fully committed or not committed at all—creates unnecessary pressure that actually prevents many people from making any changes.

The small experiment approach offers a third way: deeply engaged exploration without premature commitment. It's not half-hearted; it's precisely targeted. It respects both your desire for change and the complexity of your existing life.

Silicon Valley has codified this approach through the concept of the "minimum viable product"—the smallest version of an idea that can still deliver value and generate learning. In your midlife journey, you can adopt the same paradigm through minimum viable life changes: the smallest shifts that might meaningfully impact your satisfaction.

What would this look like in practice? If you're considering a major career pivot, perhaps you start with a side project rather than a resignation letter. If you're contemplating moving to a new city, maybe you arrange a month-long stay before selling your house. If you're drawn to a creative pursuit, you might commit to a daily practice for 30 days before restructuring your schedule around it permanently.

Little-known research from organizational psychologist Herminia Ibarra supports this incremental approach. In her study of successful midlife career changers, Ibarra found that those who made sustainable transitions rarely did so through a single dramatic break. Instead, they engaged in what she calls "identity play"—trying on possible selves through extracurricular activities, side projects, and volunteer work before making larger commitments. This experimental phase allowed them to develop new skills, build new networks, and gradually shift their self-conception without the pressure of needing immediate results.

This approach isn't just practical—it's psychologically sophisticated. At 40, your identity has been shaped by decades of experiences, relationships, and choices. Attempting to suddenly become someone entirely new isn't just logistically challenging; it can create profound internal conflict and identity disruption. Small experiments allow for integration rather than revolution, evolution rather than reinvention.

Tim Ferriss, author of "The 4-Hour Workweek," popularized a version of this approach through what he calls "lifestyle design." Rather than accepting conventional paths or making blind leaps, Ferriss advocates for systematic testing of alternative approaches to work and life. His recommendation of "mini-retirements"—extended breaks taken throughout one's career rather than saved for the end—exemplifies the small experiment mindset. Instead of waiting decades to discover if a particular lifestyle suits you, you can sample it now, learn from the experience, and incorporate those insights into your current reality.

Gail Honeyman's novel "Eleanor Oliphant Is Completely Fine" offers a powerful fictional example of how small changes can accumulate into profound transformation. The protagonist doesn't dramatically reinvent herself overnight; she makes incremental shifts in her habits and perspectives that gradually expand her world. It's a reminder that transformation doesn't require theatrical gestures—sometimes it's as simple as saying yes to a new experience or altering a single habit.

The beauty of small experiments is that they accommodate the messiness of real life. Few of us at 40 have the luxury of completely starting over without consideration for financial obligations, family responsibilities, or community ties. But almost everyone can carve out space for controlled experiments that honor both their yearning for change and their existing commitments.

This is where midlife uncertainty becomes an advantage rather than a liability. Your uncertainty is simply information—it tells you where experimentation is needed. Rather than seeing your questions as evidence of failure, you can reframe them as the beginning of inquiry. Each small experiment becomes not a do-or-die proposition but one data point in an ongoing exploration.

James Clear, author of "Atomic Habits," offers a mathematical perspective that makes the case for small changes even more compelling. He notes that if you improve just 1% each day, after a year you'll be 37 times better. This "compound interest" of small improvements applies not just to skills but to self-knowledge. Each small experiment builds on the last, creating an increasingly refined understanding of what brings you alive.

There's a little-known concept from computer science that applies beautifully here: "gradient descent." It's an algorithm that finds solutions by taking small steps in the direction of improvement, constantly evaluating and adjusting. The power of this approach is that it doesn't require knowing the entire path in advance—just the next small move toward something better. Your midlife journey can follow the same pattern: you don't need to see the entire future, just the next experiment that might yield useful information.

Some of the most significant innovations in human history have come not from grand visions perfectly executed but from small experiments that yielded unexpected results. Alexander Fleming discovered penicillin because he noticed something unusual in a failed experiment. The Post-it Note emerged from a "failed" attempt to create a super-strong adhesive. The microwave oven was invented after Percy Spencer noticed a chocolate bar melting in his pocket while working with radar equipment.

Your life at 40 is no different. The path forward may emerge not from perfect planning but from paying attention to the results of small experiments—especially the unexpected ones.

Consider the story of Marco Williams, who at 41 was a successful but increasingly dissatisfied attorney. Rather than dramatically quitting law, Williams created a small experiment: he took a two-week vacation to volunteer on a habitat restoration project, something entirely outside his normal experience.

"I didn't go into it thinking it would change my career," Williams recalls. "I just knew I needed something different in my life, and this was as different as I could imagine."

The experience didn't lead Williams to abandon law for environmental work, as one might expect in a more simplistic narrative. Instead, it awakened his interest in tangible, physical results—seeing actual change happen in the landscape over time. This insight led to his next experiment: seeking out legal cases with more tangible outcomes. Within a year, he had shifted his practice to focus on land use and environmental law, where he could visit the sites affected by his work and see concrete results.

"I never would have made that connection without the experiment," Williams notes. "I didn't need a whole new career—I needed a different relationship with the one I had."

Small experiments also allow for what psychologists call "psychological safety"—the ability to take risks without fear of devastating consequences. When the stakes of change are lowered, creativity flourishes. You can try approaches that might seem too risky in an all-or-nothing context.

This brings us to perhaps the most important advantage of small experiments: they allow for failure. And failure, despite its negative connotations, is the most efficient teacher we have. When you conduct small experiments, you can fail quickly, cheaply, and with minimal disruption to your core stability. Each failure provides information that narrows the field of what might work for you.

The pressure of midlife often creates the illusion that we should know exactly what we want and precisely how to get it. Small experiments offer liberation from this impossible standard. They allow you to say, "I don't know yet, but I'm finding out"—a stance that's not just more honest but ultimately more productive than pretending certainty.

So if you're 40 and unsure, resist the urge to make dramatic, irreversible changes based on untested assumptions. Instead, become a scientist of your own experience. Design small, bounded experiments that can yield information about what truly engages you. Pay attention to the results, especially the surprising ones. Let each experiment inform the next.

This approach isn't about thinking small—it's about learning big through manageable risks. It honors both who you've been and who you might become. It recognizes that at 40, you bring decades of wisdom to the process of change, wisdom that deserves better than a blind leap into the unknown.

The question isn't "What should I do with the rest of my life?"—a question so large it paralyzes. Instead, ask, "What small experiment might teach me something useful today?" This isn't settling for less; it's setting yourself up for discovery.

Your life at 40 isn't waiting for one dramatic transformation. It's ready for thoughtful evolution, one small experiment at a time.

5 - Stop Asking "What's My Purpose?"

The question haunts cocktail parties, late-night journal entries, and therapy sessions of the midlife unsure: "What is my purpose?" We ask it with the gravity of philosophers and the desperation of the lost. We read books promising to help us "discover our why." We take assessments designed to reveal our "true calling." We listen to podcasts where successful people describe the moment they found their North Star. And yet, for many of us at 40, the answer remains frustratingly elusive—a phantom that appears just real enough to chase but never solid enough to grasp.

What if we've been asking the wrong question all along?

The entire premise of finding your purpose assumes something profound: that purpose exists independently of you, waiting somewhere to be discovered—a pre-ordained path with your name etched into its stones. This assumption runs deep in our cultural mythology. We speak of people being "born to" do certain things. We romanticize the lightning-bolt moment of clarity when someone "found their calling." We treat purpose as a lost object—something we misplaced but might stumble upon if we search diligently enough.

This framing isn't just misleading—it's paralyzing. It turns the act of living meaningfully into a high-stakes treasure hunt where you either find the one right answer or remain perpetually incomplete. It suggests that until you discover this purpose, you're merely killing time, existing in the waiting room of your real life.

Here's a radical thought: What if purpose isn't found but created? What if it doesn't announce itself with trumpets and clarity but emerges quietly through action, engagement, and the choices you make each day?

The existentialists understood this decades ago. Jean-Paul Sartre famously proposed that existence precedes essence—we are thrown into the world first, and only through our actions and choices do we create who we are. There is no predetermined "human nature" or purpose waiting to be discovered; instead, we define ourselves through what we do. This isn't just philosophical theory—it's liberating practical wisdom for anyone at 40 still waiting for purpose to arrive with a set of clear instructions.

Friedrich Nietzsche, another existentialist thinker, suggested something even more provocative: perhaps meaning isn't discovered but imposed. We create meaning through our willingness to assert value in a world that doesn't come with values pre-installed. This isn't a pessimistic view but an empowering one—it places the authority to determine what matters squarely in your hands.

More recently, behavioral economics has provided scientific backing for what the existentialists intuited. Our preferences and sense of meaning aren't as stable or pre-existing as we imagine. They're remarkably fluid, shaped by context, experience, and—most importantly—our own actions.

Dan Gilbert, a Harvard psychologist, has shown through his research that humans have a "psychological immune system" that helps us find satisfaction in our choices after we've made them. His studies reveal that people who make irreversible decisions often end up happier than those who maintain the option to change their minds. Why? Because once we commit to a path, our brains get to work constructing meaning and value around that choice.

The implication is profound: meaning often follows action rather than preceding it. You don't necessarily need to identify your purpose before engaging deeply with life. Instead, purpose can emerge from engagement.

A little-known study conducted by psychologists at the University of Missouri tracked people's sense of purpose over a ten-year period. The researchers expected to find that those who reported a strong sense of purpose at the beginning would show better life outcomes at the end. Instead, they discovered something surprising: having a sense of purpose wasn't nearly as important as engaging in purposeful behavior. People who regularly took actions that contributed to others or developed their own capacities reported higher well-being—regardless of whether they could articulate an overarching "purpose" guiding those actions.

This research suggests a simple but powerful reversal: instead of waiting to discover your purpose so you can act purposefully, try acting purposefully to discover your purpose.

The implications are liberating. You're released from the pressure of needing to identify the one perfect path before taking a step. Instead, meaning can emerge from any activity approached with intention, care, and connection to something beyond yourself.

Michael Thompson exemplifies this reversal. At 41, Thompson was a mid-level account manager at a marketing firm, divorced with two young sons he saw on weekends. By conventional measures of purpose—career advancement, groundbreaking achievement, world-changing impact—his life might have seemed ordinary. His job was stable but not particularly fulfilling. His most significant responsibility outside work was coaching his sons' soccer team—something he'd volunteered for simply because the previous coach had moved away.

"It started as just something I did because it needed doing," Thompson explains. "There was no lightning bolt, no sense that I was fulfilling my destiny. The team needed a coach, and I had played soccer in high school. That was it."

But over time, something unexpected happened. The weekend hours spent on muddy fields with squirming eight-year-olds became the most meaningful part of Thompson's life. Not because he discovered he was "meant to be" a youth soccer coach—but because the activity itself generated meaning through its impact.

"I started noticing changes in the kids—not just in how they played, but in how they treated each other, how they responded to challenges. One boy who could barely make eye contact at the beginning of the season was high-fiving teammates by the end. Another who would cry with frustration when he missed a shot learned to shake it off and keep playing."

Thompson didn't find meaning in a job title or a dramatic life change. He created it through showing up consistently for something that initially seemed mundane. The purpose emerged from the action, not the other way around.

This pattern appears repeatedly when you look closely at lives rich with meaning. Purpose rarely announces itself in advance. More often, it accumulates gradually through engagement with ordinary activities that create value for others or connect us to something larger than ourselves.

Behavioral scientist Nicholas Epley's research at the University of Chicago provides another window into this process. Epley studies "social cognition"—how we think about and connect with others. His work reveals that meaningful social connection doesn't require grand gestures. Simple actions—genuine conversation with a stranger, small acts of kindness, expressing gratitude—create significant well-being. The catch? We consistently underestimate how good these small connections will make us feel.

The same principle applies to purpose. We imagine that meaningful work requires grand scale or dramatic impact, overlooking how ordinary actions accumulate into a life of significance. The hospice volunteer who sits with the dying, the neighbor who organizes the community garden, the parent who reads bedtime stories—none might claim to have found their cosmic purpose, yet each creates meaning through sustained engagement with what's directly before them.

The novelist George Eliot captured this truth beautifully in "Middlemarch" when she wrote of her protagonist that "the effect of her being on those around her was incalculably diffusive: for the growing good of the world is partly dependent on unhistoric acts." Meaning often resides not in what makes headlines but in what makes a difference to those within our reach.

This view challenges our cultural obsession with purpose as something exceptional, dramatic, or unique to each individual. Perhaps what we call purpose is less about discovering a singular calling and more about bringing purposefulness to whatever we do.

Viktor Frankl, psychiatrist and Holocaust survivor, proposed that humans can create meaning in three primary ways: through work or creative deeds, through experiencing something or encountering someone, and through the attitude we take toward unavoidable suffering. Notably absent from his framework is any suggestion that we must identify one specific avenue of meaning predestined for us individually.

Instead, meaning becomes available in nearly any circumstance—if we approach life with the right orientation. Frankl wrote, "Life ultimately means taking the responsibility to find the right answer to its problems and to fulfill the tasks which it constantly sets for each individual." Purpose, in this view, isn't a single answer but an ongoing response to life's evolving questions.

This approach dissolves the anxiety many feel at midlife about having missed their purpose or taken a wrong turn. If purpose is created rather than found, then it's never too late to begin creating it. The question shifts from "What was I meant to do with my life?" to "What meaning can I create from where I am now?"

This reframing connects to a little-known concept called "job crafting," developed by organizational psychologists Amy Wrzesniewski and Jane Dutton. Their research reveals how people in even the most seemingly routine jobs can create meaning by reshaping their work to align with their values and strengths. Hospital cleaners, for instance, can see their work as merely sanitizing spaces—or as creating healing environments crucial to patient recovery. Same job, radically different experience of purpose.

The lesson extends beyond the workplace: we have more power to craft meaning in our existing circumstances than we typically recognize. Purpose doesn't require dramatic external changes so much as internal reorientation and intentional engagement.

This doesn't mean you should remain in situations that crush your spirit or contradict your values. Sometimes major changes are exactly what's needed. But it does suggest that meaning-making is always available, regardless of circumstances—a power that resides within you rather than in finding the perfect external fit.

For those at midlife feeling they've somehow missed their purpose, this perspective offers profound relief. You haven't failed to find your purpose—you've simply been operating under a flawed premise about how purpose works. It's not a pre-existing destination but a capacity you develop through engagement with what matters.

This view also challenges another common assumption: that purpose must be singular. Many people torture themselves trying to identify their "one true calling," as though meaning comes only in concentrated form. But what if purpose is more like a mosaic than a monolith—composed of multiple sources of meaning that may shift and evolve throughout life?

Anthropologist Mary Catherine Bateson proposed the concept of "composing a life" to describe how meaning emerges not from following a single linear path but from weaving together disparate elements into a coherent whole. In her studies of women's lives in particular, Bateson observed that significance often emerged from combinations of roles and commitments that might seem unrelated from the outside but created a rich tapestry of meaning for the individual living them.

This mosaic model of purpose relieves the pressure to find the one perfect answer to the "what should I do with my life" question. Instead, purpose might come partly from your work, partly from relationships, partly from creative pursuits or community involvement—with the proportions shifting across different life seasons.

Psychologist Brian Little offers a complementary perspective through his research on "personal projects." Little suggests that meaning emerges not from abstract notions of purpose but from the concrete projects we undertake—from raising children to learning an instrument to improving a neighborhood. These projects connect us to values and communities larger than ourselves, creating purpose through engagement rather than philosophical declaration.

This project-based view of purpose has practical implications: if you're feeling adrift at midlife, the answer may not be to search harder for your cosmic purpose but to commit more deeply to projects that engage your capacities and contribute to others. Purpose emerges in the doing.

A compelling example comes from the world of medicine. A 2009 study published in the Journal of the American Medical Association followed a group of surgeons who performed cleft palate repair in developing countries. These physicians had established careers at prestigious institutions but described their volunteer surgical work— often performed under challenging conditions with limited resources—as the most meaningful aspect of their professional lives. Notably, few had set out with this purpose in mind; most had simply agreed to join a colleague on a trip. The profound meaning they discovered emerged from the experience itself, not from a prior sense of calling.

This pattern—deep meaning emerging unexpectedly from action taken for more modest or practical reasons—appears repeatedly in stories of purposeful lives. The environmental activist who initially just wanted to clean up the local park. The social entrepreneur who started by solving a problem that affected their family. The artist who began creating simply because they enjoyed the process, with no grand vision of cultural contribution.

In each case, purpose wasn't waiting fully formed to be discovered. It evolved through engagement, expanding as the individual recognized the value their actions created.

This evolutionary view of purpose aligns with what psychologists call an "emergent strategy" approach to life planning. Rather than charting a complete course based on predicted outcomes, emergent strategy involves taking a step, seeing what happens, learning from the results, and then determining the next step. Purpose reveals itself gradually through this iterative process.

The alternative—what we might call the "blueprint approach" to purpose—assumes we can and should design our complete life path in advance. This works wonderfully in architecture but often fails spectacularly in human lives, where conditions change, opportunities emerge unexpectedly, and our own preferences evolve in ways we couldn't have predicted.

At 40, you have the advantage of knowing this truth experientially. Think back to what you wanted at 20 or 30—how many of those desires still resonate? How many new sources of meaning have entered your life that you couldn't have anticipated? The pattern is clear: purpose evolves. Treating it as fixed ignores the beautiful adaptability of human meaning-making.

This evolutionary perspective transforms the midlife question from "What is my purpose?" to "What creates meaning for me now, and how might I move toward more of that?" The first question assumes a static, pre-existing answer; the second acknowledges meaning as dynamic and co-created between you and your environment.

So if you're 40 and still unsure about your purpose, perhaps the path forward isn't more soul-searching or personality assessments. Perhaps it's deeper engagement with what's already before you, combined with experimental steps toward what intrigues you. Purpose may be less something you find than something you forge through sustained attention and action.

This doesn't mean lowering your ambitions or settling for less meaningful work. Quite the opposite—it means recognizing that meaning-making is a capacity you already possess, one that can transform ordinary activities into sources of profound purpose.

The divorced father coaching soccer. The account manager mentoring new hires. The neighbor organizing the community garden. None might claim to have found their cosmic purpose, yet each creates meaning through bringing full attention and care to what's directly before them.

What if that's not the consolation prize for failing to find your grand purpose, but the very substance of a purposeful life?

When we look closely at lives rich with meaning, we rarely find people who discovered a pre-existing purpose and then lived it out like following a script. Instead, we find people who brought purposefulness to their circumstances —who created meaning through how they engaged with the world before them.

That capacity doesn't diminish with age or depend on having made perfect choices in your younger years. It's available now, wherever you are, however uncertain you might feel about your larger direction.

So stop asking what your purpose is, as though it exists independently of your actions. Start asking what creates meaning for you now, what allows you to contribute value, what engages your unique capacities. Then do more of that, with greater intentionality and care.

Purpose isn't waiting to be found. It's waiting to be created —by you, from exactly where you stand today.

6 - Quit Faster

We have a peculiar relationship with quitting in our culture. We venerate persistence, celebrating those who push through adversity with gritted teeth and stubborn resolve. Perseverance becomes a virtue unto itself, regardless of what's being persevered through. "Winners never quit," we're told from childhood. "Quitters never win." The message is clear: abandoning a pursuit—any pursuit—marks you as lacking something essential: grit, commitment, or moral fiber.

By the time we reach 40, this messaging has usually calcified into an unquestioned truth. We've accumulated degrees we don't use, maintained friendships that stopped nourishing us years ago, and perhaps remained in careers that drain our energy day by day. Why? Not because these choices continue to serve us, but because we've internalized the belief that walking away equals failure.

What if this entire framework is backward? What if quitting—strategic, intentional quitting—is not the mark of weakness but a profound strength? What if learning to quit faster and more skillfully is exactly what you need at midlife to create space for what truly matters now?

The most damaging myth about quitting is that it represents a single act—a moment of weakness or surrender. In reality, not quitting is the passive choice. Continuing requires nothing but inertia. True quitting, by contrast, is active. It demands courage, clarity, and the willingness to disappoint others and even parts of yourself. Far from being easy, quitting what no longer serves you may be among the most difficult skills to master.

Yet few of us ever develop this skill. Instead, we remain trapped by a psychological tendency that behavioral economists call the "sunk cost fallacy"—our irrational tendency to continue investing in something based on what we've already invested, rather than on its future potential. The more time, money, energy, or identity we've sunk into a path, the more tenaciously we cling to it, even when all evidence suggests it's time to move on.

This fallacy warps our decision-making in profound ways. We stay in unfulfilling careers because we've already invested years climbing the ladder. We continue degree programs that no longer align with our interests because we've already completed three semesters. We maintain relationships that drain us because we've already invested so much emotional energy. In each case, we're making decisions based on backward-looking accounting rather than forward-looking potential.

Researchers Daniel Kahneman and Amos Tversky illuminated this tendency through their groundbreaking work on cognitive biases. They discovered that humans are naturally loss-averse—we feel the pain of losses more acutely than the pleasure of equivalent gains. Quitting activates this loss aversion with brutal efficiency. When we quit, we make tangible the "loss" of whatever we've invested, transforming it from a vague opportunity cost into a concrete forfeiture.

This psychological trap affects even the most analytically minded. A study conducted at MIT revealed that even trained economists—people who explicitly understand the irrationality of honoring sunk costs—still fell prey to the fallacy when making personal decisions. The pull of past investments clouded their judgment despite their theoretical knowledge.

The myth of persistence creates another trap at midlife: the assumption that what you've already built must form the foundation of what comes next. We believe our future options should capitalize on our existing investments rather than potentially rendering them obsolete. This insidiously narrows what feels possible just when we might benefit most from a broader horizon.

Author and entrepreneur Seth Godin captures this dilemma perfectly in his concept of "the dip"—that painful stretch between beginning something and mastering it. Godin argues that strategic quitting isn't about avoiding difficulty but about distinguishing between "the dip" (temporary challenges on the path to mastery) and "the cul-de-sac" (situations where no amount of effort will yield the desired outcome). The real failure, in his framework, isn't quitting but continuing to invest in cul-de-sacs while opportunities for genuine growth pass by.

This distinction illuminates a truth rarely acknowledged in our persistence-obsessed culture: quitting isn't the opposite of success. It's often a prerequisite for it.

Consider Jeff Bezos, who in 1994 was a rising star at D.E. Shaw, a prestigious Wall Street hedge fund. At 30, with no background in technology or retail, Bezos recognized the potential of the internet and made a decision that baffled many of his colleagues—he quit. He walked away from a lucrative finance career to start an online bookstore in his garage. That decision to quit arguably created more value than any act of persistence could have in his original path.

This pattern of strategic quitting preceding remarkable success appears repeatedly when you look closely at accomplished lives. Toni Morrison spent years as an editor at Random House, nurturing other authors' work, before publishing her own first novel at 39. Had she not eventually quit prioritizing others' writing to focus on her own, the literary world would have lost one of its most profound voices.

Sara Blakely worked selling fax machines door-to-door for seven years before quitting to launch Spanx with her $5,000 savings. Vera Wang was a figure skater, then a Vogue editor for 17 years before quitting to become a bridal wear designer at 40. In each case, what we celebrate as success required first the courage to quit something that was merely good to make space for something potentially transformative.

But these dramatic examples of quitting leading to extraordinary achievement can actually reinforce another harmful myth—that quitting is only justified if it leads to spectacular outcomes. This creates an impossible standard that keeps many people stuck in situations that have ceased to serve them. The truth is that quitting often creates value not through what it directly enables but through what it prevents: the slow draining of energy, motivation, and possibility that comes from persisting in the wrong path.

A little-known psychological phenomenon called "goal shielding" reveals why quitting can be so transformative even without a clear next step. Researchers at the University of Rochester found that when we commit strongly to specific goals, our brains automatically suppress awareness of alternative opportunities. This mechanism helps us focus but also creates a kind of cognitive tunnel vision that prevents us from noticing possibilities outside our current path.

The implication is profound: you can't fully see what else might be possible while firmly committed to your current trajectory. Sometimes you need to quit not because you have a perfect alternative lined up, but because only by quitting can you restore your ability to perceive the full range of opportunities available to you.

This reveals the wisdom of what we might call "exploratory quitting"—walking away from what's not working without necessarily having the next phase fully mapped out. While conventional wisdom frames this as reckless, at midlife it can be surprisingly strategic. The decades of experience you've accumulated provide a safety net that wasn't available in your twenties. You know more about what works for you, what doesn't, and how to create value in the world. This hard-won wisdom makes exploratory periods less risky than they might appear from the outside.

Professional poker player Annie Duke offers a useful framework for thinking about quitting in her work on decision-making under uncertainty. Duke notes that in poker, top players focus not on avoiding folding (quitting a hand) but on folding badly played hands quickly to conserve resources for stronger opportunities. The goal isn't to win every hand but to maximize overall returns by strategically quitting hands with poor prospects.

This "quit fast, quit often" mentality runs counter to our cultural programming but aligns with how skilled decision-makers operate under conditions of uncertainty. They recognize that resources—whether chips in poker or time in life—are finite. Every moment spent in a suboptimal situation represents opportunity cost.

For those at midlife, this opportunity cost grows more acute. With your most energetic decades potentially behind you, the resource of time becomes increasingly precious. Quitting faster isn't just strategically sound—it's an acknowledgment of your own finitude and a commitment to using what remains with greater intention.

But quitting well requires more than just recognition of opportunity cost. It demands emotional skills rarely taught or celebrated. Chief among these is the ability to disappoint —both others and parts of yourself that have become attached to a particular identity or path.

Harvard developmental psychologist Robert Kegan speaks of "immunity to change"—the complex ways we protect ourselves from the discomfort of transformation. According to Kegan, we develop elaborate psychological systems that simultaneously express a commitment to change while also preventing it. These competing commitments often center around avoiding disappointment, shame, or the disorientation of identity shifts.

Quitting challenges these immunities directly. It requires disappointing the part of yourself that once chose this path and believed in it. It may require disappointing others who have come to define you by your existing commitments. It demands moving toward discomfort rather than away from it—a capacity that typically strengthens with age but rarely without conscious cultivation.

This emotional dimension explains why even people who intellectually understand the sunk cost fallacy still struggle to quit effectively. The barriers aren't primarily cognitive but emotional and identity-based. You're not just walking away from a situation; you're walking away from a version of yourself that chose and invested in that situation. This requires a grief process rarely acknowledged in discussions of strategic quitting.

A less discussed aspect of effective quitting is what we might call "identity continuity"—the ability to maintain a coherent sense of self across transitions. When we've deeply identified with a role, relationship, or pursuit, quitting can create a crisis of self-definition. Who am I if not the person who does this work, lives in this place, or maintains this relationship?

The skill lies not in avoiding this identity disruption but in developing sufficient internal stability to weather it. This stability comes not from external markers of success or specific achievements but from what psychologists call "narrative coherence"—your ability to tell a meaningful story about your life that accommodates both continuity and change.

At 40, you have the advantage of a longer life narrative to work with. You can recognize patterns in your own history that transcend specific roles or pursuits—consistent values, approaches to problems, or ways of relating that persist even as external circumstances change. This narrative flexibility allows you to quit specific situations without experiencing it as quitting "who you are."

Irish author Samuel Beckett captured this paradox beautifully in his famous line: "Ever tried. Ever failed. No matter. Try again. Fail again. Fail better." The wisdom lies not in avoiding failure but in failing forward—using each iteration to refine your understanding of what doesn't work and thereby narrow the field of what might.

Viewed through this lens, quitting becomes not an admission of defeat but a form of success—the successful completion of a learning cycle that now allows you to reallocate resources more wisely. You haven't failed; you've succeeded in discovering that this particular path doesn't lead where you want to go.

This perspective runs counter to how quitting is typically framed in professional contexts. We're encouraged to explain gaps in our resumes as anything but conscious choices to walk away. We construct elaborate narratives about "new opportunities" or "seeking challenges" rather than simply acknowledging that we recognized a mismatch and had the wisdom to exit. This dishonesty perpetuates the stigma around strategic quitting and prevents others from benefiting from our hard-won insights about when to walk away.

What would change if we began celebrating skilled quitting as much as we celebrate persistence? What if our professional profiles highlighted not just what we've built but what we've had the wisdom to abandon? What if we recognized that the ability to say "this isn't working for me anymore" represents emotional intelligence rather than inconstancy?

For those at midlife, this reframing offers particular liberation. You've likely accumulated obligations, identities, and commitments that made sense in earlier chapters but may now constrain more than they enhance. The question becomes not whether you should quit some of these but which ones and how.

The how of quitting deserves more attention than it typically receives. Quitting needn't be dramatic or absolute. Sometimes the wisest quit is a partial withdrawal—reducing investment rather than eliminating it entirely. This might mean moving from full-time to part-time in a career that no longer fully engages you but still offers value.

It might mean shifting a friendship from weekly dinners to occasional check-ins when the relationship no longer holds the same centrality.

These partial quits allow you to preserve what remains valuable while creating space for new possibilities. They acknowledge the reality that few things are entirely worth continuing or entirely worth abandoning. Most exist in the messy middle where discernment rather than absolutes is required.

But some situations do warrant complete exits, and recognizing these requires clarity about your non-negotiables—the conditions without which continued investment makes no sense regardless of sunk costs. These vary by individual and context, but they often center around core values, health impacts, or fundamental misalignments that no amount of adjustment can resolve.

Identifying these non-negotiables becomes easier at midlife as your self-knowledge deepens. You've likely experienced enough to recognize the difference between situational challenges that can be worked through and fundamental mismatches that no amount of effort will resolve. This wisdom is hard-earned and should be trusted, especially when it suggests it's time to quit.

The timing of quitting also matters more than is commonly acknowledged. Quitting too early can mean missing the growth that comes through persisting through difficulty. Quitting too late means wasted resources and diminished opportunities elsewhere. The sweet spot lies in quitting just as the marginal return on continued investment begins to clearly decline—not when the situation becomes unbearable.

This optimal quitting point arrives sooner than most people recognize. By the time you're certain you should quit, you've typically already stayed too long. This is why developing the habit of regular, honest assessment is crucial. Rather than waiting for a breaking point, consider establishing periodic review points where you candidly evaluate whether each significant commitment continues to align with your values, goals, and circumstances.

At 40, you've likely developed enough pattern recognition to trust your intuition in these assessments. When something consistently drains more energy than it provides, when your enthusiasm requires increasingly elaborate self-talk to maintain, when you find yourself having the same frustrations repeatedly without resolution —these are signals worth heeding earlier rather than later.

The barriers to heeding these signals are often social as much as psychological. We fear judgment from others who may interpret our quitting as lack of commitment or grit. We worry about disappointing those who have come to rely on us in our current roles. We dread the conversations explaining our decisions to bosses, partners, friends, or communities who may not understand or support our choice to exit.

These social pressures are real but often exaggerated in our minds. Most people are far more absorbed in their own journeys than in judging yours. Those who react with judgment to your quitting often do so not from genuine disapproval but from the discomfort your choice triggers about their own unexamined commitments. Their reaction reflects their relationship with quitting more than their assessment of your specific situation.

As for those who genuinely depend on you—partners, children, team members, communities—the question becomes not whether your quitting impacts them but whether the cost of your continuing outweighs that impact. Sometimes the most responsible choice for all involved is to stop persisting in situations that drain your capacity to contribute meaningfully elsewhere.

The ultimate skill in quitting well lies in transforming it from an act of rejection to an act of selection. You're not just quitting something; you're choosing something else— even if that something else is initially just space, possibility, or the absence of what wasn't working. This reframing shifts quitting from a negative to a positive act, from walking away from to walking toward.

At 40, with potentially decades of productive life ahead, the wisdom to quit faster what doesn't serve you isn't giving up —it's refusing to give up on what might still be possible if you create the space for it to emerge. It's recognizing that the true failure isn't in walking away from paths that no longer serve but in clinging to them at the expense of paths that might.

So quit faster. Not everything. Not recklessly. But strategically, intentionally, and without the shame our persistence-obsessed culture tries to attach to the act of stopping. Your future self, with limited time and energy remaining, will thank you not for what you stubbornly finished but for what you had the wisdom to abandon when the continuing no longer made sense.

The paths not taken don't represent failure. They represent the price of the path you choose instead. Make that choice with eyes open to both what you're leaving and what you're making space to discover. In that clarity of choice lies the freedom that midlife uniquely offers—if you have the courage to quit what's merely good to make space for what might yet be transformative.

7 - Your Job Isn't Who You Are (Anymore)

At dinner parties, there's that moment. The silence after someone asks, "So, what do you do?" Your answer comes automatically, rehearsed from a thousand introductions. Your title. Your company. Your industry. A neat package tied with the bow of professional identity. But what happens when that package no longer fits? When the label you've worn for decades starts to feel like someone else's name tag stuck to your chest?

Here we are at forty—or forty-adjacent—and something profound is happening. The script is changing. The audience is different. And most importantly, the actor—you—is questioning whether this is even the right play.

The truth hides in plain sight: your job was never who you were. But our culture performs an elegant sleight of hand, replacing your whole being with your economic function. We become what we repeatedly do to pay bills, and somewhere along the way, the provisional arrangement calcifies into identity.

Now is the time to peel them apart.

Richard had been at Goldman Sachs for seventeen years. His business cards impressed everyone. His bonus could buy small houses. When people asked what he did, their eyes widened appropriately. But on a Tuesday evening in

March, four days after his forty-second birthday, Richard stood in his Manhattan kitchen realizing he couldn't remember his nine-year-old daughter's favorite color. He'd missed her school play the previous week—market volatility had demanded his presence elsewhere. His son's baseball trophies sat on a shelf he barely glanced at.

Richard isn't real—at least not as a single person. He's a composite, drawn from interviews with dozens of high-achieving professionals who reached midlife and found themselves wealthy in capital but impoverished in presence. But his story illuminates a pattern so common that it borders on cliché: the successful professional who wakes up to find they've traded time for money so efficiently that their life has become an afterthought to their career.

This isn't just about workaholism. It's about identity theft—the silent kind we perform on ourselves.

"I realized I had become a banker who occasionally visited his family, rather than a father who happened to work in finance," one former Wall Street executive told me. Three months later, he took a seventypercent pay cut to work at a community bank ten minutes from his home. "My kids recognized me again. Not just physically—they remembered who I was as a person."

Organizational psychologist Amy Wrzesniewski has spent decades researching how people relate to their work. Her research reveals three primary orientations: job, career, or calling. Those with a "job" orientation see work purely as a means to an end—income to support life elsewhere. The "career" orientation focuses on advancement and achievement. But it's the "calling" orientation that's most seductive—and potentially most dangerous. When work becomes a calling, it can swallow every other part of your identity.

The trouble begins when a calling becomes both compass and map—directing not just what you do, but who you believe yourself to be.

Ancient craft traditions understood something we've forgotten. Medieval guilds—associations of artisans who controlled the practice of their craft—recognized that even the most dedicated worker was more than their profession. Guild members were certainly defined partly by their work—they were silversmiths, wheelwrights, coopers—but they lived multidimensional lives within communities that valued them beyond their productive capacity. Their crafts were expressions of their humanity, not replacements for it.

The industrial revolution changed everything. As philosopher Erich Fromm observed, modern work increasingly transformed humans from beings who used tools into tools themselves. We became human resources—fungible assets rather than irreplaceable souls. The digital economy only accelerated this transformation, with terms like "human capital" masking the uncomfortable reality that we've become investments expected to yield returns.

All of which brings us to your LinkedIn profile—that carefully curated highlight reel of professional accomplishments that supposedly represents your worth to the world. At forty, it's worth asking: does that digital CV reflect who you are, or merely what you've been paid to do?

James Hollis, the Jungian analyst, suggests that the first half of life is necessarily about establishing ego, security, and social identity—often through work. But the second half requires a profound reorientation toward authenticity and meaning. "The fundamental question of midlife," Hollis writes, "shifts from 'What does the world want from me?' to 'What does the soul want from me?'"

Your soul, notably, does not care about your job title.

The physicist Alan Lightman tells a little-known story about the great Albert Einstein. While Einstein's name is synonymous with genius, his personal correspondence reveals something surprising. In 1902, unable to find an academic position after graduation, Einstein took a job as a patent clerk—a position well below his intellectual capabilities. Yet in letters to friends, he expressed genuine appreciation for this arrangement, noting that the routine work left his mind free for contemplation. While processing patent applications by day, his mind wandered through thought experiments about relativity. His "day job" wasn't his identity—it was simply the economic arrangement that made space for his deeper work.

During those years as a patent examiner, Einstein published four papers that revolutionized physics. His career wasn't his purpose; it was merely the structure that supported it.

This pattern appears repeatedly throughout history. William Carlos Williams, one of America's most influential poets, worked as a family physician in Rutherford, New Jersey for over forty years. He wrote poetry between patient visits, scribbling lines on prescription pads. When asked about this apparent double life, Williams rejected the premise. "No one believes that I'm a poet and a doctor," he once remarked. "They say, 'You're a doctor who writes poetry.' No. I'm a poet who practices medicine."

The distinction matters. Williams didn't see medicine as his core identity and poetry as a hobby. He recognized himself primarily as a poet who happened to earn his living through medicine. The economic function didn't define him—it enabled him.

Not everyone needs such dramatic separation between vocation and income. But everyone needs the psychological freedom to distinguish between what they do for money and who they fundamentally are.

At forty, this distinction becomes urgent. The structures that once seemed so solid—career ladders, professional milestones, institutional affiliations—reveal themselves as the provisional arrangements they always were. Your company won't love you back. Your profession can't attend your funeral. Your resume won't hold your hand in the hospital.

A peculiar liberation comes with this realization.

The untethering of identity from occupation creates space for a more expansive self to emerge. This doesn't necessarily mean you should quit your job tomorrow (though for some, that might be exactly the right move). Rather, it means recognizing that your job—whether you love it, tolerate it, or hate it—is simply one facet of your existence, not its defining characteristic.

A profound study from Harvard's Grant & Glueck research —one of the longest-running longitudinal studies of human development—found that professional success ranked surprisingly low among factors predicting life satisfaction and well-being. What topped the list? Quality relationships. Not just romantic partnerships, but deep connections across multiple spheres of life—family, friendship, community. The research suggests that at forty, diversifying your identity portfolio may be the wisest investment you can make.

Consider the research of Laura Carstensen at Stanford University, whose socioemotional selectivity theory suggests that as time horizons shrink—as we become more aware of life's finitude—we naturally prioritize emotionally meaningful goals over achievement-oriented ones. This isn't a crisis or failure; it's an evolutionary adaptation. Your changing relationship to work at midlife isn't evidence of professional burnout—it's evidence of emotional intelligence.

There's something both humbling and exhilarating about realizing you've been playing a part that no longer fits. The humble part acknowledges that much of what you've been chasing may have been constructed from external expectations rather than internal desire. The exhilarating part is the recognition that you can set down roles that have become too heavy to carry.

In the 1970s, there was an obscure pottery teacher named Mark Brighton who taught at a community college in Vermont. Brighton had trained at prestigious arts institutions and harbored ambitions of gallery showings and artistic recognition. But at forty-three, after years of rejection letters and commercial indifference to his work, he made a decision that seemed like surrender: he took a full-time teaching position and reduced his "serious" artistic practice to evenings and weekends.

What happened next doesn't fit our cultural narratives about career and identity. Brighton didn't become famous. His work never hung in major galleries. But something else occurred—something so subtle most people would miss it. He began making the best work of his life. Without the pressure of commercial validation, his pottery developed a quality of presence that attracted devoted students and a small but passionate collector base.

More importantly, according to those who knew him, Brighton himself transformed. The slumped shoulders and furrowed brow gave way to an easy laugh and genuine attention to those around him. "I stopped being a frustrated artist," he later wrote in a local arts journal, "and became a whole person who makes art." Brighton lived another thirty-four years, teaching generations of students while producing work that, while never famous, possessed an authenticity that commercial success couldn't have conferred.

The story contains no dramatic pivot, no headline-worthy transformation. Brighton didn't quit to climb mountains or start a revolutionary business. He simply stopped identifying primarily as "a potter" and recognized himself as a person whose life included, among other things, making pottery. The shift was internal, nearly invisible—and completely transformative.

At forty, we stand at a crossroads similar to Brighton's. The path forward isn't about dramatic reinvention so much as recalibration—recognizing that we've been carrying weight that was never ours to bear.

Think of the business cards in your wallet or the title beneath your email signature. These are useful fictions, convenient shorthand for economic transactions. They are not your epitaph. They are not even the most interesting thing about you.

The most valuable question you can ask yourself now isn't "What should I do next in my career?" but rather "Who am I beyond my economic function?" The answers may surprise you—and they'll certainly prove more durable than any professional identity.

This untethering doesn't happen easily. Our economic systems are designed to keep us identified with our productive output. Consumer culture bombards us with messages linking personal worth to professional achievement and subsequent purchasing power. Even well-meaning questions from friends and family—"So how's work going?"—reinforce the primacy of career in our identity construction.

Resisting these forces requires both awareness and community—finding others who see you as more than your business card. It means deliberately cultivating aspects of self that have nothing to do with economic productivity. The hobby pursued without hope of monetization. The relationship nurtured without networking potential. The skill developed purely for the joy of development.

Early in his career, the psychologist Viktor Frankl noted a curious phenomenon among his patients. Those who defined themselves primarily through their professional identities were significantly more vulnerable to existential crises when those identities were threatened. Loss of a job, career setbacks, or forced retirement often triggered profound depression in such individuals. Meanwhile, those with more diversified sources of meaning demonstrated remarkable resilience in the face of professional disruption.

Frankl wasn't suggesting that work couldn't be meaningful—his own career brought him great satisfaction. Rather, he was observing that when work becomes the primary container for meaning and identity, that container proves dangerously fragile.

Your job may end. Your career may change. Your professional identity will inevitably shift. But you remain.

There's a beautiful resilience in this recognition—a durability that transcends performance reviews and market fluctuations. When you no longer outsource your identity to your occupation, you reclaim something essential: the authority to define yourself on your own terms.

This doesn't mean work can't matter deeply. It doesn't mean you shouldn't take pride in what you create and contribute. It simply means recognizing that your job—even if it's a true calling—is something you do, not someone you are.

At forty, this distinction offers liberation from expectations that may have served their purpose but now constrain more than they enable. The question shifts from "Am I successful enough in my career?" to "Is my life rich enough in meaning?"

That richness rarely comes from a single source. It emerges from the tapestry of connections, contributions, curiosities, and compassions that constitute a fully inhabited life. Your job might be a significant thread in that tapestry—perhaps even a central one—but it isn't the entire cloth.

When we peel professional identity from personal essence, something remarkable happens: work often improves. Freed from carrying the entire weight of our self-worth, our labor can become more playful, more creative, more genuinely productive. We bring our whole selves to work rather than expecting work to create our whole selves.

The greatest irony may be this: loosening your grip on professional identity doesn't diminish your contribution—it enhances it. When work becomes something you do rather than someone you are, you bring more presence, more creativity, and more humanity to the endeavor. You show up as a person, not a function.

At forty, you've earned this perspective. You've logged enough hours in enough roles to know that no single occupation could possibly contain the fullness of who you are. You've developed enough wisdom to recognize that the business card in your wallet represents a convenient fiction, not an existential truth.

Your job isn't who you are. It never was. And in that recognition lies not disappointment, but freedom—the freedom to be more fully alive than any job title could ever capture.

8 - There's No Medal for Exhaustion

You've seen them—those walking badges of honor. The colleague with perpetually bloodshot eyes who boasts about their fourth consecutive all-nighter. The friend who rattles off their impossible schedule like it's a résumé. The acquaintance who hasn't taken a vacation in three years and wears it like a Purple Heart. They speak of exhaustion with a strange pride, as if perpetual depletion were an achievement rather than a warning.

Perhaps you've been them. Perhaps you are them.

We live in a culture that has confused tiredness with worthiness, busyness with importance, and exhaustion with excellence. Somewhere along the way, we began measuring our value by how depleted we allow ourselves to become. The frazzled, overcommitted, sleep-deprived human has been elevated to aspirational status—the living embodiment of dedication.

But here's the uncomfortable truth: there is no medal for exhaustion. No ceremony awaits where you'll be recognized for the most emails answered at midnight or the most weekends sacrificed. No one is keeping score of how many times you pushed through when your body and mind begged for rest.

At forty, this realization can hit with particular force. You've spent decades playing by these unspoken rules, accumulating fatigue like interest on a debt. The returns diminish while the costs compound. Your body speaks in new languages—pain where there was resilience, slowness where there was speed. Your mind, once capable of cognitive gymnastics on minimal sleep, now demands proper care. This isn't weakness or decline—it's wisdom finally outpacing conditioning.

Our glorification of exhaustion isn't natural; it's manufactured. The industrial revolution introduced a profound shift in human consciousness—time became currency, and human output became measurable. The assembly line wasn't just a physical reality but a philosophical one, teaching us that our worth could be quantified by production. Digital technology only accelerated this framework. Now, with our devices ensuring we're perpetually available, the assembly line follows us everywhere, from our beds to our dinner tables to our vacations.

The result is a peculiar form of cultural madness: we exhaust ourselves to earn money to pay for recovery from the exhaustion caused by earning the money. The ouroboros of modern productivity swallows its own tail, and we call this achievement.

The science tells a different story. A fascinating longitudinal study from NASA, rarely cited outside specialized journals, examined the relationship between work hours and productivity over an extended period. The findings contradict our culture's assumptions: after approximately 50 hours of work per week, productivity not only plateaus but actively declines. For knowledge workers, the optimal range appears even lower—around 35-40 hours maximizes both output quality and cognitive function. Beyond these thresholds, the law of diminishing returns becomes the law of negative returns.

Yet we continue to valorize those who ignore these biological realities, praising their "dedication" while overlooking the mediocre quality their exhaustion produces. We applaud effort over outcome, hours over impact, suffering over results.

In the quiet moments, when no one is watching and no praise is forthcoming, a question emerges: What if all this exhaustion—this perpetual, prideful depletion—isn't actually serving you? What if, instead of proving your worth, it's diminishing your life?

The Hungarian psychologist Mihaly Csikszentmihalyi spent decades studying optimal human experience, ultimately developing the concept of "flow"—that state of complete immersion in a challenging but manageable task. His extensive research revealed something counterintuitive: our best work, our most creative solutions, and our deepest satisfaction rarely emerge from states of exhaustion. Instead, they come from the delicate balance of engagement without depletion, challenge without overwhelm.

Most striking in Csikszentmihalyi's findings was the role of recovery. Flow states—those periods of highest productivity and creativity—were sustainable only when punctuated by genuine rest. Without this rhythm of engagement and recovery, performance deteriorated and psychological wellbeing suffered. The implications are clear: rest isn't what happens when you're done working—rest is what makes good work possible in the first place.

This isn't merely theoretical. In the 1920s, a little-known industrial experiment transformed our understanding of productivity. The Western Electric Company's Hawthorne Works commissioned research on how working conditions affected output. The initial focus was on lighting levels, but researchers soon discovered something unexpected: regular rest periods dramatically improved both productivity and accuracy. When workers were given brief, intentional breaks throughout the day, their total output increased while errors decreased.

Nearly a century later, we're still resisting this wisdom. We pride ourselves on powering through, pushing beyond limits, operating on empty. We've confused endurance with effectiveness, mistaking the ability to withstand unnecessary suffering for strength.

Legendary trainer Phil Maffetone, who has coached world-class endurance athletes for decades, observed a pattern among his most successful clients. The differentiating factor wasn't who trained the hardest or endured the most pain. It was who recovered most effectively. The champions weren't those who pushed hardest but those who balanced intense effort with deliberate restoration. In endurance sports, this principle is now widely accepted. In everyday life, we still celebrate those who never rest.

The real tragedy isn't just that we're exhausting ourselves without reward. It's that we're missing what becomes possible when we stop.

There's a little-known story about the painter Henri Matisse that illustrates this principle beautifully. In 1941, Matisse underwent a difficult operation that left him bedridden and unable to paint as he had before. Forced into a period of rest and recovery, he began experimenting with paper cutouts—a technique that required less physical exertion than traditional painting. What emerged from this period of enforced rest wasn't diminished work but an entirely new artistic direction. Art historians now consider his cutouts among his greatest contributions to modern art —vibrant, free, and expressive in ways his earlier work had not been. His period of rest didn't end his creativity; it transformed it.

What might be waiting on the other side of your exhaustion?

At forty, we've internalized decades of messages equating worth with depletion. These beliefs don't surrender easily. They've been reinforced by everything from performance reviews to social media, from cultural heroes to economic systems. But what if the most courageous act isn't pushing through but stepping back? What if wisdom isn't found in enduring unnecessary suffering but in questioning why we've normalized suffering in the first place?

The neuroscience of rest reveals something our productivity culture would prefer we didn't know: your brain doesn't actually shut off when you rest. It shifts. While your conscious mind relaxes, your default mode network activates, processing experiences, making connections, and solving problems beneath the surface of awareness. Some of your most valuable mental work happens precisely when you stop trying to be productive.

This explains why solutions often appear during a shower, a walk, or upon waking from sleep. The breakthrough emerges not despite the pause but because of it. Rest isn't the absence of productivity—it's a different kind of productivity, one our metrics fail to capture but our results reveal.

Perhaps the most radical notion: what if rest isn't something you earn but something you take because it's rightfully yours? What if rest isn't the reward for work but a fundamental human need, as essential as food or water? What if you don't need to justify rest any more than you need to justify breathing?

A quiet revolution is brewing against the cult of exhaustion. Companies like Basecamp have experimented with four-day workweeks and strict boundaries around working hours. Their counterintuitive finding? Productivity remained stable or improved, while worker satisfaction and retention dramatically increased. Similarly, when Microsoft Japan tested a four-day workweek, productivity jumped by 40%, alongside significant decreases in costs related to office maintenance and employee burnout.

These examples suggest something profound: much of our exhaustion isn't necessary or even useful. It's habitual and cultural, maintained by inertia rather than necessity or results.

But organizational policy is only part of the picture. The deeper shift must happen within—in our identity, our self-worth, our definition of a life well-lived. This is where, at forty, you have a particular advantage. You've accumulated enough life experience to know that following unconscious scripts leads to predictable outcomes. You've seen the toll of exhaustion on yourself and others. You're old enough to question the wisdom of depleting yourself for external validation yet young enough to create decades of different choices.

The most insidious aspect of exhaustion culture is how it disconnects us from ourselves. When perpetually depleted, we lose access to our internal signals—those quiet messages about what we truly need, desire, and value. Exhaustion becomes both habit and hiding place, keeping us too busy to face the questions that matter. What do I really want? What is enough? What kind of life am I creating?

These aren't questions that can be answered in stolen moments between meetings or in the fog of sleep deprivation. They require presence, reflection, and the courage to sit with uncertainty—all impossibilities in a state of chronic depletion.

Artist and writer Ingrid Fetell Lee tells a story about a period when she was struggling with burnout while writing her first book. After months of diminishing returns—longer hours producing fewer usable pages—she reluctantly took a two-week break. No writing, no research, no productivity whatsoever. She spent days walking in nature, sleeping abundantly, seeing friends, and engaging in activities solely for pleasure. When she returned to her manuscript, something had shifted. The work that had felt leaden now flowed. Ideas that had been forced now arrived unbidden. In two weeks after her rest, she produced more quality work than in the two months of exhaustion preceding it.

This pattern—enforced rest leading to improved rather than diminished output—appears so consistently across domains that we might call it a natural law rather than an anomaly. The question isn't whether rest improves performance but why we continue to resist this truth.

Part of the answer lies in fear. In a culture that conflates busyness with importance, rest can feel like risking irrelevance. If I'm not constantly producing, proving, and performing, will I still matter? If I'm not exhausted, am I doing enough? These fears aren't irrational in systems designed to measure value by visible output and perpetual availability.

But beneath these practical concerns lies something deeper—a question of identity and worth. Who am I when I'm not producing? What is my value beyond what I accomplish? These existential questions lurk beneath our crowded calendars and midnight emails, questions we're too exhausted to confront.

At forty, you've earned the right to answer differently. You've accumulated enough evidence that exhaustion-as-lifestyle leads nowhere worth going. You've witnessed the toll of depletion on health, relationships, creativity, and joy. You're standing at a crossroads where continuing down the familiar path of depletion leads to predictable consequences, while the alternative remains largely unexplored.

What would it mean to declare that there is no medal for exhaustion, and even if there were, you would respectfully decline to compete for it?

It might mean establishing boundaries that protect your energy rather than constantly overriding your limits. It might mean detaching your sense of worth from your level of depletion. It might mean measuring success by the quality of your presence rather than the length of your to-do list.

Most radically, it might mean recognizing that rest isn't something you need to earn but something you already deserve by virtue of being human.

This isn't about abandoning ambition or commitment. It's about recognizing that sustainable excellence requires sustainable energy. It's about distinguishing between the work that matters and the performative exhaustion that doesn't. It's about creating space for life to happen not despite your work but alongside it.

Imagine approaching the second half of life not as a sprint toward some elusive finish line but as a deliberate journey with alternating periods of engagement and recovery. Imagine treating your energy as your most valuable resource—more precious than money, more limited than time. Imagine valuing presence over productivity, depth over breadth, meaning over metrics.

This shift doesn't happen overnight. The habits of exhaustion run deep, reinforced by social approval and economic systems. But it begins with a simple recognition: There is no medal for exhaustion. No prize awaits the most depleted. The rewards you're chasing through chronic depletion—recognition, security, significance—remain eternally out of reach precisely because exhaustion diminishes the very qualities needed to attain them.

The alternative isn't laziness or disengagement. It's strategic renewal—the deliberate practice of replenishing your physical, emotional, mental, and spiritual resources. It's saying no to depletion so you can say yes to what truly matters. It's recognizing that your energy, not your time, is your most precious currency, and spending it accordingly.

At forty, you stand at a crucial inflection point. The habits of your first four decades have created momentum that, left unexamined, will carry you through the next four. The scripts you've followed—consciously or not—have shaped your relationship with work, rest, and worth. Now is the time to ask whether these scripts are leading you toward the life you want or merely the life you've been conditioned to pursue.

The good news? You're not starting from scratch. You've accumulated wisdom, perspective, and self-knowledge that weren't available to your younger self. You've seen enough of life to recognize patterns and consequences. You're old enough to question cultural assumptions yet young enough to chart a different course.

The path beyond exhaustion isn't marked by less meaningful work but by more purposeful rest. It's distinguished not by lowered standards but by sustainable excellence. It's characterized not by disengagement but by deliberate presence.

There's no medal for exhaustion. There never was. But there is a life waiting on the other side of perpetual depletion—one with space for depth, joy, creativity, and contribution that emerges not from proving your worth through suffering but from offering your gifts from a place of wholeness.

That life doesn't require another decade of depletion to earn. It's available now, beginning with the radical act of believing that your worth isn't measured by your exhaustion—and never was.

9 - You Can Be Bad at It and Still Love It

The first time Sarah Bennett uploaded a video to her YouTube channel "Medieval Morsels," she spent fourteen hours researching, cooking, filming, and editing. She carefully reconstructed a 15th-century English recipe for "compost," a vegetable preserve mentioned in ancient household manuals. The lighting was poor, her narration awkward, and the final dish looked nothing like modern preserves. After two weeks, the video had garnered exactly seven views—four of which were from her immediate family.

By conventional metrics of success, Sarah's debut was an abject failure. Yet three years and over one hundred videos later, she still films weekly, rarely breaking a hundred views on any single upload. Her small kitchen in suburban Minnesota has become a laboratory where medieval cooking techniques come alive, if only for a viewership that could fit comfortably in a studio apartment.

When asked why she continues despite the minimal audience, Sarah—a dental office manager by day—smiles and says, "I'm probably the world's worst medieval cooking YouTuber. But every Thursday night, I get to time travel. How could I give that up just because I'm not good at it?"

Sarah's story might seem merely charming, possibly even a bit sad to those steeped in metrics of success and audience growth. But hidden within her weekly ritual lies a revolutionary defiance against one of our era's most suffocating orthodoxies: the belief that activities are only worth pursuing if we excel at them or can leverage them into something "productive."

At forty, this belief system has likely cost you countless hours of potential joy. How many experiences have you declined because you wouldn't immediately be good at them? How many interests have you abandoned at the first sign of mediocrity? How many pleasures have you denied yourself because they wouldn't contribute to your resume, your status, or your sense of measurable progress?

Our culture has developed a peculiar relationship with skill acquisition. We've normalized the expectation that adults should only engage in activities where they demonstrate immediate aptitude or clear potential for mastery. The casual pickup basketball game has given way to the optimized training regimen. The weekend painting class has surrendered to the carefully curated Instagram portfolio. The kitchen experiment has been replaced by the sous vide precision of social media-worthy results.

Even our language betrays this mindset. We speak of "killing time" or "guilty pleasures"—phrases that position unoptimized enjoyment as either wasteful or shameful. We've been conditioned to believe that if an activity isn't making us better, smarter, more skilled, or more employable, it must be justified through some other means

—usually through its contribution to productivity elsewhere in our lives.

"I run because it clears my head for work." "I play piano to improve cognitive function." "I cook to save money on restaurants."

Rarely do we grant ourselves permission for the simplest, most human justification: I do this because I enjoy it, regardless of my skill level.

This wasn't always the case. Throughout much of human history, amateurism—from the Latin "amator," meaning lover—was not just accepted but celebrated. To be an amateur was to engage in an activity purely for the love of it, without concern for professional standards or external validation. The Victorian era saw an explosion of amateur naturalists, musicians, astronomers, and archaeologists who contributed significantly to their fields while maintaining day jobs as clergymen, housewives, doctors, or civil servants.

Charles Darwin, whose theory of evolution revolutionized biology, was essentially an amateur naturalist for much of his life. His voyage on the Beagle was undertaken not as a professional scientist, but as a companion to the ship's captain with an intense curiosity about the natural world. His lack of formal scientific training might have even benefited his work, allowing him to approach questions from unorthodox angles.

Somewhere along the way, we lost this tradition. The professionalization of everything, coupled with social media's amplification of exceptional talent, has squeezed out the space for beloved mediocrity. When everyone's highlight reel is constantly on display, the joyful amateur feels increasingly anachronistic.

Psychologist Ellen Langer's groundbreaking work on mindfulness offers an intriguing explanation for why being bad at something we love can actually enhance rather than diminish the experience. In her studies, Langer found that when people focus on the process rather than outcomes— on the doing rather than the achieving—they not only enjoy activities more but often show surprising improvements that elude those fixated on results.

In one fascinating experiment, Langer had amateur musicians perform pieces either with instruction to focus on technicalities and perfection or to simply notice something new and enjoy the process. Audiences consistently rated the latter performances as more technically proficient and artistically compelling, despite the musicians focusing less on skill. The secret? When we engage playfully rather than perfectionally, we access flow states more readily and bring our full presence to the activity.

This finding challenges everything our achievement-oriented culture teaches. What if the path to enjoyment— and sometimes even to unexpected mastery—isn't through striving for excellence but through embracing the possibility of mediocrity?

The reality is that at forty, you're likely already quite good at several things. Your professional skills, parenting abilities, social navigation—these have been honed through decades of practice and feedback. But this competence can become a cage when it establishes the expectation that everything you do must meet similar standards of excellence.

Breaking free from this cage might be one of midlife's most liberating possibilities. What awaits on the other side isn't a descent into apathy or an embrace of failure, but rather the rediscovery of play, exploration, and joy untethered from outcome.

The neurological benefits of this shift are substantial. When we engage in activities with no pressure to perform at high levels, our brains release different neurochemicals than during achievement-oriented tasks. The stress hormones that accompany performance anxiety decrease, while dopamine and serotonin—associated with pleasure and satisfaction—increase. This cocktail creates ideal conditions for learning, creativity, and most importantly, enjoyment.

Professor Stuart Brown, founder of the National Institute for Play, has documented how play states—those experiences characterized by apparent purposelessness, voluntary engagement, inherent attraction, freedom from time, diminished consciousness of self, and continuation desire—are not just enjoyable but essential to cognitive and emotional health. His research suggests that playful engagement, regardless of skill level, provides cognitive, emotional, and even physical benefits that more structured, achievement-oriented activities often cannot.

Yet many adults, particularly those in midlife, find themselves play-deprived. The demands of careers, families, and social expectations leave little room for activities that can't be justified through their contribution to productivity or self-improvement. When play does occur, it's often rationalized as "stress relief" or "mental health maintenance"—valuable purposes, certainly, but distinctions that miss the fundamental nature of play as its own reward.

The courage to be bad at something—to embrace amateurism in its purest sense—becomes a radical act in this context. It challenges the premise that our value lies in our utility, productivity, or excellence. It reclaims spaces of experience that haven't been colonized by the logics of capitalism, optimization, or personal branding.

There's a little-known story about the physicist Richard Feynman that beautifully illustrates this principle. Despite being one of the most brilliant scientific minds of the 20th century, Feynman developed a passionate interest in drawing and painting in his 40s. He studied with artist Jirayr Zorthian and produced hundreds of sketches and paintings throughout his later life, none of which approached the technical skill of his scientific work.

When asked why he devoted so much time to an activity at which he showed modest talent, Feynman replied, "I don't have to be good at it. I'm not trying to be a professional painter. There's no such question as why." For Feynman, the experience of creating art—the noticing, the curiosity, the engagement with color and form—was sufficient justification for the pursuit, regardless of the outcome.

This attitude reflects what philosopher Bernard Suits called "the lusory attitude"—the willingness to accept unnecessary obstacles for the sake of making an activity possible. In his influential book "The Grasshopper: Games, Life and Utopia," Suits argues that play involves "the voluntary attempt to overcome unnecessary obstacles." When we golf, for instance, we deliberately make the simple task of placing a ball in a hole vastly more difficult by using specialized sticks and arbitrary rules. The unnecessary difficulty creates the experience.

Applied to midlife pursuits, the lusory attitude offers a revolutionary framework. What if the point isn't to become good but to engage fully? What if the obstacles, the learning curve, the awkwardness, and even the failures are not impediments to the experience but constitutive of it?

Caroline Knapp, in her essay "Making the Most of the In-Between," writes about taking up rowing in her late thirties despite having no natural athletic talent. She describes how the very difficulties—the blisters, the frustration, the slow progress—created a relationship with the activity that transcended conventional notions of achievement: "I row not because I'm good at it but because I'm not. Because it's hard and humbling and forces me outside myself."

At forty, this perspective offers particular resonance. You've lived long enough to recognize that many paths lead to fulfillment, that conventional markers of success often fail to deliver their promised satisfaction. You've also accumulated enough life experience to weather the ego bruises that come with being a beginner, with producing mediocre results despite earnest effort.

What's more, you likely possess something your younger self could not: the capacity to appreciate process over product. To find value in the doing itself, regardless of outcome. This shift in perspective doesn't happen automatically with age, but it becomes available in ways that youth, with its urgent need for validation and achievement, often prohibits.

The social dimensions of embracing beloved mediocrity shouldn't be underestimated. When we give ourselves permission to be bad at things we love, we implicitly extend that permission to others. This creates spaces where connection happens through shared joy rather than competitive comparison. The amateur pottery class, the community theater production, the casual sports league—these environments foster a different quality of human relationship than spaces organized around excellence and achievement.

Researchers at the University of Michigan found that adults who regularly participated in amateur activities reported stronger community connections and lower levels of social isolation than those whose activities were primarily professional or achievement-oriented. The shared vulnerability of being not-very-good together created bonds that perfectionism often precludes.

This finding aligns with what sociologist Ray Oldenburg called "third places"—social environments separate from home and work where people gather primarily for enjoyment and community. Historical examples include pubs, cafes, community centers, and churches. In contemporary life, amateur pursuits often create these third places, offering connection not through what we produce or achieve, but through what we enjoy together.

The financial implications of embracing amateurism are equally significant. When freed from the expectation of excellence, activities require far less investment. The beginning painter doesn't need professional-grade supplies. The amateur musician doesn't need the finest instrument. The recreational tennis player doesn't need private coaching or top-tier equipment.

This democratization of enjoyment runs counter to contemporary consumer culture, which often correlates serious engagement with significant spending. Industries profit from our belief that proper participation requires proper gear, proper training, proper attire—all defined by increasingly specialized standards of adequacy. The amateur, by contrast, makes do. Improvises. Works within limitations rather than struggling to transcend them.

There's a poignant economic freedom in this approach. At forty, with financial responsibilities often at their peak, the ability to derive profound enjoyment from activities that don't drain resources becomes not just philosophically appealing but practically necessary.

The most surprising benefit of embracing beloved mediocrity may be its effect on the areas where you do strive for excellence. When your identity and self-worth no longer depend entirely on professional achievement or specialized mastery, those pursuits themselves often improve. The pressure diminishes. The desperate grip on outcomes loosens. The playfulness that characterizes your amateur endeavors begins to infuse your professional ones.

Psychologists call this "psychological flexibility"—the ability to move between different modes of engagement depending on context. Those who can alternate between achievement-oriented focus and process-oriented enjoyment demonstrate greater resilience, creativity, and overall life satisfaction than those locked into a single approach.

A little-known study from the California Institute of Creativity tracked mid-career professionals who maintained regular amateur pursuits alongside their professional work. The findings showed that those with dedicated amateur interests—regardless of their skill level in those activities—demonstrated greater problem-solving abilities, adaptability to change, and overall job satisfaction than peers whose activities all aligned with their professional identities.

The implications for age forty and beyond are profound. As career paths become less predictable, economic security more tenuous, and traditional markers of success more questionable, the ability to derive genuine fulfillment from activities divorced from achievement becomes not just a philosophical nicety but a practical necessity.

So what might embracing beloved mediocrity look like in practice? It begins with permission—the explicit acknowledgment that being bad at something you love is not just acceptable but potentially valuable. This permission extends to time as well as performance; amateur pursuits deserve space in your schedule not because they contribute to productivity elsewhere but because enjoyment itself matters.

It continues with community—finding or creating spaces where the joy of the activity, rather than excellence in it, forms the center of gravity. These might be formal groups or informal gatherings, in-person or virtual, but their defining characteristic is an emphasis on participation over performance.

Most challenging, perhaps, it requires a recalibration of how you measure value—a willingness to assess experiences not by their outcomes or external validation but by the quality of engagement they foster. Did time disappear? Did self-consciousness fade? Did you feel fully present? These become the relevant metrics, not skill development or observable results.

None of this comes easily in a culture obsessed with optimization, productivity, and visible achievement. Swimming against these currents requires both courage and community—the fortitude to resist prevailing norms and the support of others similarly engaged.

Yet the potential rewards extend far beyond the specific activities themselves. What begins as permission to enjoy painting despite producing mediocre landscapes becomes permission to live with greater authenticity across domains. The willingness to be a bad but joyful tennis player becomes willingness to embrace other aspects of life without requiring perfection.

There's a story about the cellist Pablo Casals that captures this ethos beautifully. When asked why, at 93, he continued to practice four to five hours daily, Casals replied, "Because I think I'm making progress." The anecdote is typically used to illustrate perseverance and lifelong learning. But it contains another, subtler message: Casals continued playing not because he had achieved unparalleled mastery (though he had) but because the engagement itself—the relationship with the instrument, the music, the practice—remained vital and evolving.

This is the invitation that midlife extends: to develop relationships with activities, pursuits, and experiences that transcend conventional metrics of success. To love what you do regardless of how well you do it. To measure the value of experiences not by their outcomes but by their quality of engagement.

Sarah Bennett's medieval cooking videos may never go viral. Her reproductions of ancient recipes may never earn critical acclaim or culinary respect. But every Thursday night, her kitchen becomes a time machine, a laboratory, a playground. She steps outside the constraints of optimization and productivity that govern her daytime hours as a dental office manager and enters a space where joy requires no justification beyond itself.

At forty, surrounded by the accumulated evidence that conventional paths often lead to conventional disappointments, you stand at a unique inflection point.

The pressure to excel, to maximize, to optimize has revealed its limitations. The opportunity to reclaim spaces of experience governed by different values—play, presence, process, pleasure—presents itself with unprecedented clarity.

The question isn't whether you can afford to be bad at things you love. The question is whether you can afford not to be. In a culture that relentlessly commodifies skill and monetizes talent, the simple joy of beloved mediocrity may be the most radical act of self-reclamation available.

So pick up the paintbrush. Sign up for the dance class. Join the community choir. Dust off the skateboard. Write the terrible short story. Cook the ambitious and slightly disastrous meal. Play the instrument gathering dust in your closet. Do it badly. Do it joyfully. Do it without apology or justification.

The freedom you find may extend far beyond the activity itself. It may, in fact, illuminate everything else.

10 - Be Useful, Not Impressive

The applause fades. The lights dim. The stage that once felt electric now feels hollow and manufactured.

You've spent decades building a life that looks good from the outside—the career with the impressive title, the achievements that sound substantial when listed in your bio, the carefully curated social media presence that suggests you've figured it all out. You've chased scale, visibility, status. All the things that make others nod and say, "Wow, they've really made it."

And yet here you are at 40-something, awake at 3 AM, wondering if any of it matters.

It doesn't have to be this way. What if I told you there's a radical pivot available—one that doesn't require quitting your job tomorrow or selling everything you own? What if the shift is mainly one of intention and attention?

The most profound life reorientation at midlife might be this: stop optimizing for impressiveness and start optimizing for usefulness.

This isn't about grand gestures or dramatic exits. It's about asking a different question each morning: "How can I be genuinely useful today?" instead of "How can I appear successful today?"

When Charlie Munger, Warren Buffett's longtime business partner, was asked about his secret to a satisfying life, he didn't mention wealth accumulation or status-seeking. Instead, he offered this remarkably simple wisdom: "The safest way to try to get what you want is to try to deserve what you want." Munger, who continued working well into his 90s, believed that focusing on creating actual value—being useful—was not just ethically sound but pragmatically superior.

The obsession with impressiveness is relatively new in human history. For most of civilization, people focused on being useful to their families and communities. The village baker didn't wake up wondering how to scale his operation to impress strangers; he wondered how to make bread that would nourish his neighbors. The local mechanic didn't strategize about "personal branding"; she fixed cars so people could get where they needed to go.

Somewhere along the way, we began valuing reach over depth, scale over substance, and impression over impact. We started believing that touching a million lives lightly somehow trumps touching ten lives profoundly.

But there's freedom waiting on the other side of that belief.

I met a man named Frank at a neighborhood gathering last year. When I asked what he did, I expected the usual career summary. Instead, he said, "Mostly, I walk dogs."

I later learned that Frank had spent thirty years in finance, made his money, and then at 58, decided to become a professional dog walker. Not to start a dog-walking empire with employees and an app and venture capital. Just to walk dogs, mostly for elderly neighbors who could no longer manage their energetic pets. He charges reasonable rates, knows every dog's quirks and preferences, and has become essential to his clients' lives.

"I used to manage millions," he told me. "Now I manage poop bags. But I sleep better."

The brilliance of Frank's choice isn't that he abandoned ambition. It's that he redirected it toward usefulness rather than impressiveness. He's not less ambitious—he's ambitiously pursuing impact at a human scale.

What about you? Where in your life are you prioritizing the appearance of success over actual usefulness? Where might you be chasing scale at the expense of depth?

Consider hospice volunteers, who sit with the dying when family members need a break. They read to the patients, hold their hands, or simply provide quiet company during the final days or hours. Nothing about this work scales. Nothing about it impresses at dinner parties. Nothing about it leads to TED talks or book deals or venture funding. And yet, is there any work more essential, more profound, more useful than accompanying humans through their final transition?

Lisa Fenn, a former ESPN producer, exemplifies this principle in a different context. While working on a story about two disabled high school wrestlers in 2009, she formed a deep connection with the boys—one who was legally blind, the other who had no legs. When the cameras stopped rolling and the story won its awards, Fenn didn't move on to the next impressive assignment. Instead, she remained deeply involved in the young men's lives, becoming a parental figure, helping them navigate college applications, and even moving them into their dorm rooms. The documentary was impressive. The ongoing commitment to these young men's lives was useful.

The psychologist Martin Seligman, known for his work on positive psychology, distinguishes between a pleasant life (focused on positive emotions), an engaged life (focused on flow states), and a meaningful life (focused on using your strengths to serve something larger than yourself). His research consistently shows that the meaningful life produces the most enduring satisfaction. And what is a meaningful life if not a useful one?

Now, I'm not suggesting you abandon all ambition or that scale is inherently negative. Many valuable innovations and services reach millions because they genuinely improve lives. But the problem comes when scale becomes the goal rather than the byproduct—when we chase impressiveness for its own sake.

At midlife, many of us realize that the validation we sought in our earlier decades—the promotions, the public recognition, the metrics of external success—didn't deliver the fulfillment we expected. That's because human satisfaction has never really come from impressing others. It comes from being useful to them.

Rebecca Solnit writes about this in her essay "The Faraway Nearby," noting how the process of helping her mother move out of her family home during her mother's descent into Alzheimer's brought a strange clarity about what matters: "In emergencies, people commit acts of generosity and sacrifice for strangers; social boundaries dissolve... [revealing] another world that was always there."

This other world—the world of usefulness rather than impressiveness—has always been available to us. We just couldn't see it through the fog of status-seeking and external validation.

So how do we make this shift? How do we reorient toward usefulness in our 40s and beyond?

It begins with examining where your current work and life activities fall on the spectrum from purely impressive to deeply useful. Some questions to consider: Would you still do this work if no one ever knew it was you who did it? Does your work solve actual problems for actual people? When you talk about your work, are you more likely to cite metrics of scale or stories of impact?

The answers might be uncomfortable. That's okay. Discomfort often precedes growth.

Next, look for small ways to shift toward usefulness. This doesn't mean you need to quit your job and become a dog walker tomorrow. It might mean volunteering one afternoon a week at a local food bank. It might mean mentoring someone junior in your field with no expectation of return. It might mean checking in on an elderly neighbor or offering childcare to overwhelmed parents in your community.

Start small. Be consistent. Notice how it feels.

An intriguing study from the University of California, Riverside found that acts of kindness—a simple form of usefulness—create a positive feedback loop. When people performed acts of kindness for others, they not only boosted the recipient's mood but also experienced greater well-being themselves. More surprisingly, witnesses to these acts also received a mood boost, creating what researchers call a "kindness contagion." Usefulness, it seems, compounds in ways that mere impressiveness cannot.

At 40-something, you likely have accumulated skills, wisdom, and resources that make you uniquely positioned to be useful. You know things. You've seen systems succeed and fail. You understand human nature in ways your younger self couldn't. These assets aren't meant to be hoarded or displayed—they're meant to be deployed in service of others.

There's a forgotten concept from ancient Greek culture worth reviving here: the idea of "arete," often translated as "excellence" or "virtue." For the Greeks, arete wasn't about outshining others; it was about fulfilling your highest purpose and function. The arete of a knife is to cut well. The arete of a doctor is to heal effectively. What is your arete? What function are you uniquely designed to fulfill?

Ask yourself: What problems am I particularly well-suited to solve? Where does my unique constellation of skills, experiences, and perspective allow me to be maximally useful?

Sometimes the answer isn't grand or impressive by conventional standards. That's fine. "Usefulness" is measured by depth of impact, not breadth of recognition.

There's a story about a woman named Maggie who, after a successful career in retail management, became a crossing guard in her early 50s. She knew every child's name, remembered their birthdays, celebrated their achievements, and created a tiny moment of safety and recognition in each child's day. Twenty years later, at her retirement party, dozens of former students—now adults—returned to thank her for being the one steady, caring adult who saw them every day during turbulent childhoods.

Was being a crossing guard as impressive as being a retail executive? By conventional standards, no. Was it profoundly useful to hundreds of children over two decades? Absolutely.

Here's the beautiful paradox: when you stop trying to be impressive and focus instead on being useful, you often end up being more impressive anyway—but in ways that actually matter. The person relentlessly focused on helping others solve real problems tends to develop a reputation for effectiveness, reliability, and wisdom that far outshines the carefully curated "personal brand" of the perpetually self-promoting.

There's a particular freedom that comes with this shift. When your worth isn't tied to metrics of impressiveness—titles, income, follower counts, or public recognition—you become immune to certain types of manipulation. You can say no to opportunities that might boost your visibility but don't allow you to be genuinely useful. You can say yes to smaller, quieter forms of service that would have seemed beneath you before.

None of this means you have to abandon your career or reject all forms of ambition. It simply means redefining success around usefulness rather than impressiveness. What if your next promotion wasn't about the title but about expanded capacity to solve important problems? What if your measure of a good year wasn't income growth but impact depth?

When the Pulitzer Prize-winning journalist Katherine Boo was asked why she spent years documenting the lives of residents in a Mumbai slum for her book "Behind the Beautiful Forevers," she replied: "Very little journalism is world changing. But if change is to happen, it will be because people with power have a better sense of what's happening to people who have none." Boo wasn't chasing impressiveness; she was doggedly pursuing usefulness by making the invisible visible.

At 40-something, you've likely accumulated enough life experience to know that the markers of status you once chased haven't delivered the satisfaction you expected. You've seen enough impressive people lead hollow lives to question whether impressiveness itself was ever the right goal. And you've witnessed enough quiet heroes—the hospice volunteers, the dedicated teachers, the community organizers—to recognize that usefulness offers a more sustainable source of meaning.

So perhaps it's time to release yourself from the exhausting performance of impressiveness. Perhaps it's time to embrace the liberation of simply being useful.

The next time someone asks what you do, try describing how your work serves others rather than citing your title. The next time you contemplate a career move, ask yourself which option allows you to solve more meaningful problems, not which one sounds better at reunions. The next time you feel that familiar anxiety about whether you're "successful enough," remind yourself that history's most satisfied people weren't those who accumulated the most impressive résumés—they were those who found ways to be most useful to the people and causes they cared about.

At 40-something, you're not too late to make this shift. In fact, you're right on time. You have the wisdom to recognize the emptiness of pure impressiveness and the skills to be genuinely useful. All that remains is the courage to redirect your ambition toward what truly matters.

Be less impressive. Be more useful. And watch as life expands to meet you in this new space of authentic service.

11 - The Path Doesn't Have to Make Sense to Anyone But You

The looks on their faces say everything. That slight tilt of the head. The momentary pause. The polite smile that doesn't quite reach the eyes. Then comes the question, thinly disguised as curiosity but loaded with judgment: "But why would you want to do that?"

At 40-something, you've likely encountered this reaction more than once when sharing your dreams, pivots, or passions. The unspoken implication hangs in the air: by now, shouldn't your path make sense to others? Shouldn't it follow some recognizable trajectory that your family, friends, and colleagues can neatly categorize and approve?

This persistent pressure to explain ourselves—to justify our choices according to some invisible but apparently universal standard of progress—becomes especially acute at midlife. We've accumulated decades of identity, career investments, and others' expectations. The weight of "making sense" grows heavier with each passing year.

But what if this burden isn't yours to carry? What if the most profound freedom of midlife is precisely this: the path doesn't have to make sense to anyone but you.

This isn't simply permission to be selfish or to disregard how your choices affect loved ones. Rather, it's an invitation to recognize that the logic of your path—the deep coherence of your life's direction—might be legible only to you. And that might be exactly as it should be.

When Anthony Bourdain published "Kitchen Confidential" at age 44, after decades of working in relative obscurity as a chef, few could have predicted his trajectory. A middle-aged cook with a heroin habit in his past suddenly becoming a literary sensation, then a global travel documentarian and cultural ambassador? It made no sense by conventional standards. Yet in retrospect, we can see how each element of his unusual path contributed to his unique voice and perspective. The years that might have looked like stagnation were actually incubation.

In a revealing interview years later, Bourdain reflected: "I feel like I've stolen a car—a really nice car—and I keep looking in the rearview mirror for flashing lights. But there's been nothing yet." This lingering sense of having somehow cheated the system—of having taken a path so unconventional that surely someone would come to collect him—stayed with him despite his enormous success.

How many potential Anthony Bourdains never emerge because they cannot tolerate the discomfort of that questioning glance, that subtle head tilt, that persistent need to justify a path that doesn't fit neatly into society's approved categories of progress?

The philosopher Søren Kierkegaard, writing in the 19th century, anticipated this modern predicament with uncanny precision. He distinguished between what he called the "aesthetic" and "ethical" stages of life, and ultimately advocated for what he termed the "religious" stage—though this had little to do with organized religion. For Kierkegaard, this highest stage meant embracing the deeply personal, even absurd nature of authentic choice. He wrote that "the supreme paradox of all thought is the attempt to discover something that thought cannot think."

In simpler terms: the most meaningful path may be precisely the one that cannot be fully justified through rational explanation to others. Its logic may be deeply personal, intuitive, or even apparently contradictory when viewed from the outside.

Tyler Perry's story embodies this paradox. Before becoming a Hollywood mogul, Perry lived in his car intermittently for six years while attempting to stage his plays. He endured multiple show failures and faced constant rejection. By conventional wisdom, his persistence defied rationality. Who continues pursuing a creative career after years of homelessness and failure? Who refuses to "get realistic" after so much struggle?

Yet Perry followed his own internal compass, even when it made no sense to anyone else. In a 2019 BET Awards speech, he reflected: "While everybody else is fighting for a seat at the table, I'll be down in Atlanta building my own." The path that seemed irrational to others—continuing to write and produce plays for a predominantly Black audience when mainstream success seemed impossible—ultimately created an entirely new model for entertainment success.

The issue isn't just about career pivots or creative pursuits. It extends to how we structure our days, our relationships, our approaches to parenting, our spiritual practices, and our definitions of success. At every turn, midlife presents opportunities to finally step off the escalator of external approval and onto the winding footpath of personal truth.

The narrative psychologist Dan McAdams has studied how people construct coherent life stories across decades. His research reveals something fascinating: those who report the greatest sense of well-being aren't necessarily those whose lives would appear most logical or successful to outside observers. Rather, they're individuals who have developed what he calls "narrative coherence"—the ability to see connections and meaning across seemingly disparate life experiences, even ones that include significant setbacks.

In other words, the path that seems random, disordered, or even unsuccessful from the outside may possess a profound internal logic that only its traveler can fully appreciate. Your winding road might not translate easily to a linear resume or dinner party introduction, but that doesn't diminish its integrity or value.

A striking example comes from the world of athletics. The great Cuban high jumper Javier Sotomayor spent years developing an unconventional jumping technique that coaches and competitors alike criticized as inefficient and technically flawed. Yet this supposedly "incorrect" approach ultimately allowed him to set a world record of 2.45 meters (8 feet, 0.25 inches) in 1993—a record that astoundingly still stands today, more than three decades later. Had Sotomayor bowed to external judgment about the "right way" to high jump, he might never have discovered the unique approach that perfectly suited his particular body and mind.

What might be your equivalent of Sotomayor's unorthodox jump—the approach that defies convention but works uniquely well for you? What activities, schedules, relationships, or pursuits might flourish if you stopped trying to make them comprehensible to others?

The pressure to justify our paths becomes particularly intense at midlife crossroads. After decades of education, career-building, and possibly raising children, society expects us to continue on established trajectories. The narrative should be one of ever-increasing stability, status, and certainty. To suddenly introduce ambiguity, exploration, or radical change at 40-something seems to violate an unwritten contract.

We see this in the language used to describe midlife transitions: "crisis," "breakdown," "reinvention." All imply something gone wrong, something that needs correction or explanation. Rarely do we speak of midlife exploration as natural evolution or rightful reclamation.

The novelist George Eliot (the pen name of Mary Ann Evans) published her first novel at age 40, after years as a translator and editor. Critics and contemporaries struggled to categorize her work, which defied the conventions of Victorian literature. Her path—from rural girlhood to urban intellectual to scandalous "living in sin" with a married man to becoming one of the greatest novelists in the English language—followed no established template.

Yet in retrospect, we can see how each seemingly disconnected phase contributed to the profound psychological insight that characterizes her work.

Eliot herself reflected on this in "Middlemarch," perhaps her greatest novel, writing: "For the growing good of the world is partly dependent on unhistoric acts; and that things are not so ill with you and me as they might have been, is half owing to the number who lived faithfully a hidden life, and rest in unvisited tombs."

The "hidden life" Eliot describes—the internal journey that may leave no monument and win no accolades—is precisely the one whose logic remains largely private. Its value cannot be measured by external metrics or validated by public understanding.

The liberation in this is immense. When you release the need for your path to make sense to others—parents, peers, partners, children, colleagues—entire territories of possibility open before you. Questions transform from "How will I explain this?" to "Is this truly meaningful to me?"

This isn't about abandoning responsibility or community. Rather, it's about recognizing that the most responsible choice might be honoring your unique journey, even when it defies easy explanation. The greatest gift to your community might be embodying authentic choice rather than predictable conformity.

Psychological research supports this perspective. The concept of "self-concordance," developed by psychologists

Kennon Sheldon and Andrew Elliot, suggests that goals aligned with our authentic interests and values—rather than those pursued for external approval or to avoid guilt—lead to greater well-being and sustained motivation. Their studies consistently show that people who pursue self-concordant goals not only achieve more but also experience greater satisfaction from their achievements.

The path that makes sense only to you is likely the path most concordant with your deepest values and interests. It's the path most likely to sustain your energy and enthusiasm across decades. And paradoxically, it's often the path that ultimately makes the most unique contribution to others, precisely because it couldn't have been walked by anyone else.

So how do we cultivate the courage to follow such a path, especially when the pressure to justify ourselves intensifies at midlife?

First, we might practice what psychologists call "radical acceptance" of our own legitimacy as authors of our lives. This means acknowledging that no external authority—no parent, spouse, boss, friend, or society at large—possesses greater insight into your proper path than you do. While others may offer valuable perspective, the final interpretation belongs to you alone.

Next, we can develop what the philosopher Martha Nussbaum calls "narrative imagination"—the ability to see our lives as ongoing stories rather than fixed identities or accumulated credentials. This perspective allows for plot twists, character development, and unexpected turns that might seem illogical in isolation but contribute to a richer overall narrative.

We might also examine where our need for external validation originated. Often, the compulsion to make our paths comprehensible to others stems from early experiences where love or approval seemed conditional on meeting others' expectations. Recognizing these patterns can help us distinguish between necessary social accommodation and unnecessary self-limitation.

Perhaps most importantly, we can seek examples of others who have walked seemingly incoherent paths with ultimate integrity. Their stories remind us that the judgment of contemporaries rarely predicts the judgment of history—or more crucially, the judgment we ultimately make of our own lives when looking back.

The medieval mystic Julian of Norwich wrote that "all shall be well, and all shall be well, and all manner of thing shall be well." This wasn't blind optimism but a profound trust in a logic beyond conventional understanding. Similarly, we might trust that our seemingly disjointed paths contain a coherence beyond what we or others can currently recognize.

This trust doesn't eliminate doubt or difficulty. The path that makes sense only to you will likely be lonely at times. You'll face not just external questioning but internal uncertainty. You'll wonder if you've missed something obvious that everyone else can see. You'll question whether your inner compass is trustworthy when it points in directions that puzzle those around you.

These doubts aren't signs of weakness or wrongness. They're natural companions on any authentic journey. The question isn't whether doubt will arise, but whether you'll allow it to redirect you toward safer, more explainable choices.

What awaits beyond this threshold of doubt is what philosophers call "existential joy"—the profound satisfaction of living in alignment with your own deepest truth, regardless of its legibility to others. This isn't the fleeting happiness of social approval or achievement. It's the sustaining joy of integrity, of wholeness, of being fully yourself in a world that often demands conformity.

The poet Mary Oliver captured this in her famous lines: "Tell me, what is it you plan to do with your one wild and precious life?" The emphasis on "your" is crucial here. Not your parents' life. Not your peers' life. Not the life that makes for an impressive biography or obituary. Your life, with all its peculiar yearnings, unexpected talents, and singular perspective.

At 40-something, you've accumulated enough experience to know that external approval doesn't satisfy the deeper hunger for meaning. You've likely achieved at least some of the goals that were supposed to bring fulfillment, only to discover their fulfillment was temporary at best. You've seen enough of life to recognize that the most impressive-looking paths sometimes lead to the emptiest destinations.

This is precisely why midlife offers such potent opportunity for reclamation. You have both the wisdom to question conventional metrics of success and enough runway ahead to chart a course more aligned with your authentic values. You can finally prioritize internal coherence over external comprehensibility.

So the next time you encounter that tilted head, that pause, that question loaded with judgment—"But why would you want to do that?"—perhaps you might simply smile and respond: "It makes sense to me."

Because ultimately, that's the only sense that truly matters.

12 - You Can Be Both Grateful and Still Want More

There's a peculiar form of guilt that settles in around midlife—a quiet voice that whispers whenever you feel the pull toward something new, something different, something more. The voice says: "How dare you want anything else? Look at everything you already have."

At 40-something, the tally of what you've accumulated can be substantial. Perhaps there's a career with some measure of stability. A home, whether rented or owned. Relationships, some spanning decades. Maybe children or other family members who depend on you. Health, imperfect but present.

So when that restless feeling emerges—that sense that despite everything, something essential remains missing—the guilt arrives right alongside it. In a world where so many have so little, who are you to want more?

This guilt reflects one of the most persistent and damaging false dichotomies of adult life: the belief that gratitude and aspiration must be mutually exclusive. That appreciating what you have necessarily means abandoning any desire for what you don't. That contentment and ambition exist in opposition rather than in creative tension.

But what if this dichotomy itself is the problem? What if you can be both deeply grateful for your life exactly as it is and still legitimately hunger for different experiences, knowledge, connections, or contributions? What if gratitude and aspiration aren't opposing forces but complementary energies that, when integrated, create a life of both groundedness and growth?

This integration—the ability to hold seemingly contradictory truths simultaneously—represents a form of psychological flexibility that might be the most undervalued superpower of midlife. It's the capacity to embrace paradox rather than forcing complex realities into oversimplified either/or categories. And it may be precisely what you need to navigate the unique combination of accumulated wisdom and remaining possibility that characterizes life at 40-something.

The psychologist Todd Kashdan has spent years researching this capacity, which he calls "psychological flexibility." His studies reveal that people with higher levels of psychological flexibility—those able to adapt their thoughts and behaviors in response to changing situations while staying connected to their values—report greater well-being across numerous metrics. They experience less depression and anxiety, more positive emotions, stronger relationships, and greater resilience in the face of challenges.

Yet our culture rarely celebrates this flexibility. Instead, we're bombarded with messages suggesting we must choose: Be ambitious or be content. Chase dreams or appreciate reality. Disrupt or accept. The middle path—

holding both—gets lost in our addiction to simplistic narratives.

The roots of this false dichotomy run deep. Western philosophical traditions often frame opposites as inherently contradictory—you must be either this or that. Eastern traditions more commonly embrace the idea of complementary opposites, as symbolized in the yin-yang. But even without invoking specific cultural frameworks, we can recognize through lived experience that human reality rarely conforms neatly to binary categories.

In "The Book of Disquiet," the Portuguese writer Fernando Pessoa captures this beautifully: "To be discontented with oneself and yet calm, to live in discomfort and yet by choice, to stay at the crossroads but to stay there by choice... Who knows if the best philosophy isn't not to have any, and the best religion simply to endure what comes?"

Pessoa isn't advocating passivity or resignation here. Rather, he's suggesting a stance of alert presence at the crossroads—the intersection of satisfaction and seeking, of gratitude and yearning. This intersection might be precisely where the richest possibilities of midlife reside.

Take the story of Mary Leakey, the renowned paleoanthropologist. At age 46, already established in her career with significant discoveries to her name, she returned to school to earn formal qualifications in archaeology and geology. Though already respected in her field and grateful for her accomplishments, she recognized that further education would enrich her work. Her example challenges the notion that education belongs primarily to youth or that established professionals should be content with their existing knowledge base.

Leakey's choice wasn't a rejection of her previous work or an indication that she was ungrateful for her accomplishments. It was an expression of the "both/and" mindset: both appreciative of her existing knowledge and hungry to expand it. Both established in her field and still growing within it.

The same dynamic appears across countless domains. The novelist who appreciates their published works while still striving to write something better. The parent who deeply loves their teenager while sometimes longing for the freedom of child-free days. The professional who values their steady job while dreaming of entrepreneurship. In each case, gratitude and aspiration coexist not as contradictions but as complementary forces.

This complementarity becomes particularly important at midlife, when the weight of accumulated responsibilities can make any new aspiration feel like an implicit criticism of what already exists. The desire to learn sailing at 45 can feel like a rejection of the hiking hobby you've enjoyed for years. The urge to change careers can feel like betraying the colleagues who've supported you. The wish for a different living situation can seem like ingratitude for the home you've created.

But what if these new desires aren't replacements but additions? What if they represent not dissatisfaction with what is but curiosity about what else might be? What if they reflect not ingratitude but a healthy human need for continued growth?

The ability to hold this duality—to be both grateful and aspiring—isn't just psychologically healthy. It's also strategically advantageous. Gratitude grounds you in present reality, preventing the "grass is always greener" thinking that can lead to perpetual dissatisfaction. Aspiration provides the energy and direction for continued growth. Together, they create a dynamic equilibrium that prevents both complacency and restless discontent.

This balanced stance has neurological underpinnings. Research in affective neuroscience suggests that positive emotions (like gratitude) broaden our perspective and build resources, while approach-oriented states (like aspiration) energize action. Neither alone is sufficient for optimal functioning. Too much contentment without drive leads to stagnation; too much drive without contentment leads to burnout.

A striking example of this balance comes from the world of elite sports. Tom Brady, widely considered one of the greatest American football players of all time, was known throughout his career for combining intense ambition with genuine appreciation. After winning his sixth Super Bowl—an unprecedented achievement at the time—he was asked if this would finally satisfy him. His response revealed the both/and mindset: "It's great to win, but I'm already thinking about next year."

Critics might interpret this as insatiable ambition or an inability to enjoy success. But those who worked closely with Brady consistently noted his capacity to deeply appreciate each victory while remaining hungry for the next challenge. This wasn't contradiction; it was integration.

The same pattern appears in the lives of those who make significant midlife changes while maintaining gratitude for their existing circumstances. Helen Hooven Santmyer worked as a college professor and librarian for decades while quietly writing in her spare time. At age 88, her novel "...And Ladies of the Club" became a surprise bestseller. Throughout interviews following her late-life success, Santmyer expressed both deep appreciation for her decades of quiet, meaningful work and satisfaction that her literary ambitions had finally found a wider audience.

What makes this integration particularly challenging at midlife is the accumulation of sunk costs. By 40-something, you've invested significantly in particular paths, relationships, and identities. Any new direction can feel like a tacit admission that these investments were somehow mistaken—that you should have chosen differently earlier.

This fear often manifests as what psychologists call "backwards-looking regret"—the painful feeling that past choices were errors rather than necessary steps in an evolving life. But what if we reframed our relationship to our past choices? What if previous paths weren't mistakes but foundations? What if the career you're now questioning provided exactly the skills, resources, and self-knowledge you need for your next chapter?

This reframing transforms the midlife equation. Your past choices weren't wrong; they were right for who you were then and instrumental in creating who you are now. Being grateful for them doesn't mean you must continue in the same direction indefinitely. It means honoring their value while recognizing that you—like all living things—are designed to grow and change.

A powerful illustration comes from the life of Frances Oldham Kelsey, a pharmacologist and physician who, at age 46, began a new position at the FDA after years in academia. In this role, she famously blocked the approval of thalidomide in the United States, preventing thousands of birth defects. Kelsey's previous academic career wasn't a detour or mistake; it provided the scientific expertise and methodological rigor she needed for her FDA work. Her willingness to take on new challenges in midlife, combined with gratitude for her established expertise, literally saved lives.

The nurse who returns to school at 45 to study archaeology isn't rejecting nursing; she's building upon it. The decades of careful observation, ethical decision-making, and human connection that defined her nursing career will inform and enrich her archaeological work. Her gratitude for what nursing taught her coexists perfectly with her aspiration to explore new terrain.

This integration of gratitude and aspiration doesn't happen automatically. It requires intentional practice of what psychologists call "cognitive flexibility"—the ability to switch between different mental frameworks depending on the situation. Sometimes you need to focus on appreciation to counter anxiety or discontent. Other times you need to lean into aspiration to prevent stagnation or resignation. The flexibility to move between these states, rather than becoming fixed in either, constitutes a form of wisdom particularly available at midlife.

How might we cultivate this flexibility? One approach involves challenging the either/or thinking that pervades our culture. When you catch yourself framing choices in binary terms—"Either I'm grateful for my job or I explore a new field," "Either I appreciate my relationship or I desire change"—pause and replace "or" with "and." This simple linguistic shift opens space for more nuanced thinking.

Another practice involves what psychologists call "temporal distancing"—mentally projecting yourself forward in time to gain perspective on current decisions. From the vantage point of your 80-year-old self looking back, how might you view the tension between gratitude and aspiration? Would that older self encourage you to play it safe out of gratitude, or would they urge you to pursue growth while carrying your appreciation forward?

The sculptor Auguste Rodin offered a perspective that embodies this integrated approach: "Nothing is a waste of time if you use the experience wisely." This suggests that our past isn't something to either celebrate uncritically or reject entirely, but rather a resource to be mindful of as we shape our future.

The false dichotomy between gratitude and aspiration often stems from fear—fear that wanting more somehow invalidates what we have, fear that change threatens stability, fear that new directions imply past mistakes. But what if the opposite were true? What if the capacity to hold both appreciation and aspiration simultaneously reflected not confusion or ingratitude but a particularly mature form of wisdom?

This wisdom recognizes that human life isn't static but dynamic, not linear but cyclical, not either/or but both/and. It acknowledges that growth doesn't require rejection of the past but can build harmoniously upon it. It understands that the most meaningful lives often unfold not through singular devotion to one path but through the integration of diverse experiences, perspectives, and pursuits.

At 40-something, you've developed the life experience to navigate this complexity. You've weathered enough changes to know that growth doesn't threaten core identity. You've accumulated enough wisdom to distinguish between fleeting dissatisfaction and genuine calling. You're ideally positioned to practice the art of holding both gratitude and aspiration as complementary rather than competing forces.

This capacity to integrate seemingly opposing qualities extends far beyond the gratitude/aspiration dynamic. It encompasses the ability to be both strong and vulnerable, both pragmatic and idealistic, both serious and playful, both independent and connected. Each pairing represents not a contradiction to be resolved but a polarity to be leveraged—opposing forces that, when held in creative tension, generate energy and possibility.

The psychiatrist and Holocaust survivor Viktor Frankl captured this wisdom in his observation that meaningful life is found not in the pursuit of happiness itself but in devotion to something beyond oneself. This devotion requires both deep appreciation for what is and committed action toward what might be. It demands that we stand gratefully in the present while reaching toward the future.

For those at midlife questioning what to do with the decades ahead, this integrated stance offers a liberating perspective. You don't have to choose between being grateful and wanting more. You don't have to resolve the tension between contentment and aspiration. The richest life emerges not from collapsing this tension but from dancing within it—from cultivating the psychological flexibility to move fluidly between appreciation and seeking, between satisfaction and striving.

The guilt that whispers "how dare you want more" stems from a fundamental misconception: that gratitude requires permanence, that appreciation demands stasis. But what if the truest gratitude involves acknowledging the gift of each experience while remaining open to what comes next? What if wanting more doesn't negate having enough but simply recognizes that human capacity for growth, contribution, and experience is virtually limitless?

The path forward isn't about choosing between gratitude and aspiration but about weaving them together—about being firmly rooted in appreciation for what is while keeping branches extended toward what might be. This integration doesn't resolve the tension so much as transforms it from a problem into a dynamic source of energy and direction.

So yes, at 40-something, uncertain about what comes next, you can be profoundly grateful for the life you've created thus far and still legitimately hunger for different experiences, knowledge, relationships, or contributions. You can appreciate the stability you've achieved and still crave adventure. You can value the expertise you've developed and still desire to be a beginner again. You can love your life exactly as it is and still want to change it.

This isn't contradiction. It's integration. It's not confusion. It's wisdom. And it might be exactly the stance that allows your next chapter to unfold with both the groundedness of gratitude and the energy of authentic aspiration.

13 - The Best Version of You Might Still Be in Beta

In a world obsessed with finished products, polished résumés, and carefully curated social media feeds, there's something revolutionary about embracing the unfinished. At 40-something, when society expects you to be fully formed, completely developed, and thoroughly established, what if the most liberating truth is this: the best version of you might still be in beta?

The pressure to be a finished product by midlife is both pervasive and insidious. It seeps in through the language we use—"midlife," as though life divides neatly into a beginning, middle, and end rather than continuously unfolding. It manifests in the questions we're asked: "Have you settled down yet?" "What have you accomplished?" "Where did you end up?" All presupposing that by now, the becoming should be over. The being should be set.

But what incredible arrogance lies in this assumption—that human development, with all its magnificent complexity, should somehow be completed by an arbitrary point on the timeline. That the richness of human potential, the depth of human growth, should fit neatly into the first few decades, leaving the rest as mere execution of an established plan.

The tech world offers us a more honest metaphor. In software development, "beta" refers to a working but incomplete version of a program—functional enough for testing but explicitly understood to be evolving. It's not a deficient state but a necessary stage in development. The beta version isn't a failure or disappointment; it's precisely where it should be in its journey toward what it will become.

What if we applied this understanding to ourselves? What if at 40-something, rather than expecting to be "done," we recognized ourselves as advanced works-in-progress—functional in many ways, accomplished in some, but gloriously, necessarily unfinished?

The film director Robert Altman offers a striking example of beta-phase potential. Though he directed industrial films and television episodes throughout his 30s, Altman didn't create his breakthrough film "MAS*H" until he was 45. He went on to become one of America's most influential filmmakers, directing classics like "Nashville," "The Player," and "Gosford Park" well into his 70s. His innovative techniques—overlapping dialogue, improvisational acting, subversion of genre—emerged not in some brilliant early flash of genius but through decades of experimentation and evolution.

Had Altman declared himself "finished" at 40, had he believed his creative identity should be fully formed by midlife, cinema would have lost one of its most distinctive voices. Instead, he embraced continuous development, refining his artistic approach with each new project.

The tyranny of the "fully formed" ideal exerts particularly strong pressure in professional contexts. Career paths have traditionally been envisioned as ladders to be climbed in the first half of life, with the second half spent either maintaining position or beginning a slow descent. By 40-something, conventional wisdom suggests you should know exactly what you are professionally and be focused on refining rather than reinventing.

Yet this model has never aligned with how human development actually works, and it has grown increasingly disconnected from economic and social reality. The concept of "careers" as fixed, linear progressions belongs to an industrial economy that no longer exists. Today's landscape demands continuous adaptation and reinvention —precisely the capacity that a beta mindset cultivates.

Developmental psychologist Robert Kegan offers a perspective that fundamentally challenges the "fully formed by midlife" expectation. His research suggests that cognitive development continues well into adulthood, with the most complex forms of thinking—what he calls "fifth-order" or "self-transforming" consciousness—rarely emerging before midlife. This advanced cognition involves the ability to hold contradictions, recognize the partial nature of any single system of thought, and continuously revise one's own mental frameworks.

In other words, the most sophisticated forms of human thinking are typically not available until precisely the age when society expects you to be finished developing. The greatest cognitive flexibility, the most nuanced understanding, the deepest capacity for incorporating multiple perspectives—these emerge not in youth but in the decades beyond 40, provided development isn't artificially curtailed by the belief that you should already be complete.

The fear of remaining unfinished—of being perpetually in beta—often stems from a misunderstanding of what constitutes success. We've inherited a notion of success that prioritizes arrival over journey, completion over continuous development. Yet in almost every domain of human achievement, the most remarkable contributions come from those who remain perpetually in process, who continue to evolve their understanding and abilities regardless of age.

The renowned comedian Maria Bamford offers a powerful example of beta-phase persistence. At 41, after decades in comedy, Bamford's career seemed stalled. Despite her undeniable talent and distinctive voice, mainstream success had proven elusive. Rather than concluding she had reached her potential and settling for a modest career, Bamford continued refining her unique approach to comedy—incorporating her struggles with mental health, developing new character voices, experimenting with format and delivery.

For six straight months at age 41, she performed sets that often fell flat or confused audiences. She was, in essence, debugging her comedic code in real-time, in public. This willingness to remain in beta—to be publicly unfinished—eventually led to her breakthrough Netflix series "Lady

Dynamite," acclaimed stand-up specials, and recognition as one of comedy's most innovative voices.

The beta mindset isn't just about professional development or creative achievement. It extends to our emotional lives, our relationships, our understanding of ourselves. At 40-something, there's a particular temptation to believe we should have figured out who we are—that our personalities, preferences, and patterns are fixed. We should know what we like and dislike, what works for us and what doesn't, who we are fundamentally.

This fixed mindset receives reinforcement from oversimplified interpretations of personality psychology. We take tests that assign us four letters or nine numbers or sixteen categories, and we begin to treat these classifications as immutable truths rather than useful but limited snapshots of who we were at a particular moment.

The field of neuroplasticity offers a profound challenge to this fixed view. Research consistently demonstrates that the brain remains malleable throughout life, capable of forming new neural connections and pathways in response to novel experiences. While certain forms of neuroplasticity do diminish with age, others actually increase. Cognitive flexibility—the ability to adapt thinking in response to changing demands—can expand rather than contract in midlife, particularly when consciously cultivated.

This scientific understanding aligns with the lived experience of those who remain in beta throughout life. They don't become less themselves as they continue to develop; they become more fully themselves as they integrate new experiences, insights, and capacities. The beta state isn't about erasing what came before but about building upon it—adding new functions while improving existing ones.

The novelist Toni Morrison embodies this continuous development. Her first novel, "The Bluest Eye," wasn't published until she was 39, after years working as an editor. While many would consider simply publishing a well-received first novel at that age accomplishment enough, Morrison understood herself as just beginning a creative journey. With each subsequent book—"Sula," "Song of Solomon," "Beloved," and beyond—she expanded her literary range, experimented with different narrative techniques, and delved into new thematic territory.

Had Morrison considered herself "formed" after her first success, had she simply replicated her initial achievement, literature would have lost the extraordinary evolution of her artistic vision over subsequent decades. By remaining in beta—by seeing herself as developing rather than developed—she created a body of work that ultimately earned her the Nobel Prize in Literature.

The resistance to remaining in beta at midlife often stems from fear—fear of appearing uncertain in a culture that rewards confident declarations, fear of seeming lost when others appear found, fear of admitting we're still figuring things out when conventional wisdom says we should know by now. This fear can be particularly acute in professional contexts, where authority often correlates with certainty.

Yet those who have made the most meaningful contributions across domains—science, art, business, education, relationships—are frequently those who maintain what psychologists call a "beginner's mind" regardless of their accumulated expertise. They combine deep knowledge with the humility to recognize how much remains unknown, substantial skill with the willingness to continue learning.

The physicist Richard Feynman exemplified this approach throughout his career. Despite winning the Nobel Prize and becoming one of the most respected scientists of his generation, Feynman consistently emphasized the provisional nature of scientific understanding and the importance of remaining open to revision. When asked about the implications of a new discovery, he famously responded: "I think I can safely say that nobody understands quantum mechanics." This wasn't false modesty but intellectual honesty—a recognition that even at the height of his powers, he remained in beta, his understanding necessarily incomplete.

What would it mean to apply this perspective to your life at 40-something? How might your relationship to your work, your relationships, your sense of self transform if you embraced being perpetually in beta?

It might mean approaching career transitions not as admissions of failure but as natural iterations in an ongoing development process. It might mean entering new relationships or revitalizing existing ones with the understanding that your capacity for connection continues to evolve. It might mean exploring interests abandoned in youth not as regression but as expansion of your experiential database.

The beta mindset doesn't mean aimlessness or refusal to commit. Software in beta has direction and purpose; it's working toward enhanced functionality rather than randomly changing. Similarly, embracing your unfinished state doesn't mean abdicating responsibility or drifting without intention. It means bringing conscious attention to your continued development rather than assuming it should be complete.

For those whose identities have been strongly tied to achievement, the beta mindset requires a fundamental reorientation of how success is measured. Rather than evaluating yourself solely by milestones reached or accolades accumulated, you might consider a different metric: growth capacity. Are you more capable of meaningful contribution today than you were a year ago? Is your understanding of yourself and others deeper or more nuanced? Has your range of effective response to life's challenges expanded? These questions focus not on endpoint achievement but on developmental trajectory.

This reorientation can be particularly liberating for those who feel they've fallen short of early promise or expectations. The narrative of the "midlife crisis" often revolves around the painful recognition of a gap between youthful potential and midlife reality. But this narrative presupposes that potential should have been fully actualized by midlife—that the gap represents failure rather than the natural space between what has been realized so far and what might still emerge.

What if we replaced the concept of the midlife crisis with that of the midlife beta test? Rather than seeing midlife questioning as evidence of failure or regression, we might recognize it as essential diagnostic feedback—information about what's working, what needs refinement, what new functions might be developed. Just as beta testers provide invaluable data that improves software, your midlife uncertainties offer crucial intelligence for your continued development, if you're willing to receive them as information rather than indictment.

The competitive swimmer Diana Nyad offers a remarkable example of the midlife beta test transformed into late-life achievement. As a young athlete in her 20s, Nyad attempted to swim from Cuba to Florida but didn't complete the journey. For decades, she pursued other endeavors, building a career as a journalist and author. Then, in her early 60s, she returned to her earlier goal, making four unsuccessful attempts before finally completing the 110-mile swim at age 64.

What's noteworthy isn't just the accomplishment itself but Nyad's relationship to the decades between attempts. Rather than seeing her 20-something failure as defining or her intervening years as detour, she integrated everything she'd learned and experienced into her renewed pursuit. The Diana Nyad who ultimately completed the swim wasn't a resurrection of her younger self but an evolved version— one whose mental toughness, emotional resilience, and self-understanding had been developing throughout her supposedly "middle" years.

The tech metaphor of perpetual beta applies not just to individual development but to relationships as well. Our connections with others—whether romantic partners, friends, family members, or colleagues—benefit from being understood as continuously developing rather than statically defined. The relationship that worked at 30 may need significant updating to remain vital at 45, not because it was flawed initially but because the individuals within it continue to evolve.

This perspective challenges the narrative of "growing apart" that often accompanies midlife relationship challenges. Rather than seeing changes as evidence of incompatibility, the beta mindset recognizes them as calls for relational evolution—opportunities to develop new functionalities that accommodate both partners' continued growth. Just as software requires updates to remain compatible with new operating systems, relationships require conscious revision to remain vibrant as participants evolve.

The belief that we should be fully formed by midlife doesn't just constrain our sense of possibility; it actively harms our capacity for continued development. When we see ourselves as complete, we filter experience in ways that confirm existing patterns rather than facilitate growth. We dismiss new information that doesn't fit our established self-concept. We avoid experiences that might reveal our incompleteness. We reject feedback that could guide further development.

In contrast, the beta mindset creates receptivity to precisely the inputs that foster continued growth. It maintains what the psychologist Carol Dweck calls a "growth mindset" rather than a "fixed mindset." It approaches challenges as opportunities for development rather than tests of established capacity. It welcomes feedback as valuable data rather than threatening criticism.

The most insidious aspect of the "fully formed by midlife" expectation may be how it constrains joy. When we believe we should have figured out who we are and what we want by 40-something, we lose the particular delight that comes with discovery—with encountering new aspects of ourselves, with surprising ourselves through unfamiliar responses, with the continuous revelation of our own unfolding.

This joy of ongoing discovery isn't youthful immaturity repackaged for midlife. It's a more mature pleasure precisely because it's informed by substantial life experience and self-knowledge. It combines the beginner's openness to novelty with the experienced person's capacity for nuanced appreciation. It integrates the delight of fresh encounter with the contextual understanding that only time provides.

What if, then, we abandoned the narrative of midlife as a period of completion, consolidation, or crisis? What if we embraced instead a vision of these decades as a particularly rich phase of beta testing—a time when our accumulated experience combines with our remaining potential to enable development of a depth and complexity impossible in youth?

This reframing doesn't deny the real constraints that midlife often brings. Physical capacities do change. Responsibilities to others often increase. Financial and practical considerations may limit certain options. But within these parameters, tremendous scope for continued development remains—often in dimensions barely conceivable to our younger selves.

The tech world has another concept worth borrowing here: continuous deployment. Rather than developing software fully before release, many companies now update their products constantly, shipping new features incrementally as they're developed rather than waiting for comprehensive revision. This approach recognizes that functionality in the present matters alongside potential for future improvement.

Applied to midlife development, continuous deployment means living fully from where you are while simultaneously evolving. It means neither deferring life until some imagined completion nor considering development finished. It means embracing your current capacities while actively cultivating new ones. It means being both what you are and what you are becoming—not as contradiction but as complementary aspects of an integrated life.

At 40-something, uncertain about what comes next, this perspective offers particular liberation. You don't need to have everything figured out. You don't need to be fully formed. The best version of you might indeed still be in beta—not as consolation but as exciting reality. Your most meaningful contributions, your deepest relationships, your richest experiences might lie not in the past but in the ongoing unfolding of who you are becoming.

This doesn't mean ignoring or devaluing what you've already created, experienced, or achieved. The beta version builds on all prior releases. It incorporates their functionalities while expanding capacity. Your continued development doesn't negate earlier versions of yourself; it integrates and transcends them, creating something both continuous with what came before and unprecedented in its new configurations.

So perhaps midlife uncertainty isn't evidence of failure or cause for crisis. Perhaps it's simply accurate recognition of your unfinished state—your ongoing beta status. And perhaps the most liberating response isn't to frantically seek completion but to embrace continuous development, not as reluctant concession to incomplete achievement but as active participation in the endless becoming that constitutes a fully lived human life.

14 - The Point Isn't to Find What to Do With Your Life. It's to Live It

There's a question that terrorizes the minds of the uncertain forty-something more than any other: "What should I do with my life?" It echoes in the midnight hours, a ghostly visitor that arrives when defenses are down. This question haunts us because we believe it has a single, correct answer—an answer we somehow missed while everyone else found theirs. An answer we should have discovered decades ago.

Let me offer you a radical proposal: There is no answer.

Not because you're asking the wrong question, but because the question itself is built on a flawed premise. The premise is that your life is an object, a thing to be manipulated, directed, and shaped toward some endpoint called "purpose" or "meaning." The premise is that your life is something you do things with, rather than something you inhabit.

This might be the most liberating truth of midlife: You are not behind. You haven't missed anything. You aren't failing at the great game of life because you haven't yet found "the thing" to do with it.

The quest to find what to "do" with your life assumes life is a raw material waiting for you to shape it. But your life isn't clay. It's water. It's already flowing. The question isn't what to do with it—the question is how fully you're willing to be in it.

Most of us spend decades pursuing what sociologist Robert Bellah called "lifestyle enclaves"—those carefully curated collections of career achievements, relationship milestones, and material acquisitions that signal we've arrived. We chase credentials, job titles, marriage certificates, mortgages, and retirement accounts. We mistake these outer markers for inner fulfillment.

Then forty arrives. The enclave starts to feel like a museum of someone else's choosing. We look around and wonder, "Is this it? Is this all there is?"

The panic that follows—what we mistakenly call a "midlife crisis"—isn't a breakdown. It's a breakthrough. The facade is cracking. You're not losing your way—you're finally finding your way out of the maze of should-haves and supposed-tos.

Physicist Richard Feynman was once asked how he conquered complex problems that stumped everyone else. His response was startling in its simplicity: "I'm not afraid to admit that I don't know the answer." This fearless embrace of uncertainty is precisely where your hidden power lies at forty. While others cling desperately to outdated certainties, you're courageous enough to stand in the discomfort of not knowing.

The German philosopher Martin Heidegger wrote about the concept of "Dasein"—literally "being there" or "presence." It's a way of existing authentically in the world by embracing your finite nature rather than avoiding it. What if the great achievement of midlife isn't finding your perfect vocation but simply becoming more present to your own existence? What if true purpose isn't a destination but a quality of attention?

A little-known study from the University of Virginia tracked adults across four decades and found something unexpected. The people who reported the highest life satisfaction in their later years weren't those who achieved their early life goals. The happiest weren't those who found their "calling" or accumulated impressive accolades. The most fulfilled were those who maintained what researchers called "responsive engagement"—the ability to remain curious and adapt to life as it unfolded, rather than forcing it to conform to a predefined vision.

Most counsel about midlife confusion centers on fixing, solving, clarifying. The assumption is that your uncertainty is a problem. But what if your uncertainty is actually wisdom in disguise? What if not knowing is exactly where you're supposed to be?

The anthropologist Mary Catherine Bateson wrote about "composing a life"—the idea that lives aren't linear narratives but improvisational compositions. She studied women whose lives didn't follow conventional patterns and found that those who embraced discontinuity often created the most meaningful lives. Their power came not from finding the perfect path but from weaving seemingly disparate elements into a whole that made sense to them, even if it appeared chaotic to outside observers.

A former business executive named Daniel once told me about leaving his high-powered career at 43. Everyone asked what he would do next, expecting a dramatic revelation—a new company, perhaps, or a bold entrepreneurial venture. But Daniel had no plan. For months, he simply walked. Miles and miles through his city, then hiking trails, then foreign countries. People worried. His wife worried. He worried.

"But something strange happened," he said. "As I walked, I stopped trying to figure out what to do with my life and started noticing that I was already living it. The birds, the conversations with strangers, the feeling of my feet on the ground—it was all happening whether I had a plan or not."

A year later, Daniel wasn't running a Fortune 500 company or leading a nonprofit or writing a bestseller. He was teaching a few community college classes and renovating old homes with a friend. His life looked smaller from the outside but felt immeasurably larger from within. He hadn't found what to do with his life. He had found his way back to living it.

That's the secret that conventional wisdom misses: The point isn't figuring out what to do with your life. The point is showing up for it with your full attention.

Our cultural narratives about midlife are all wrong. We've been told it's a crisis, a last chance, a final opportunity to correct course before it's too late. But what if midlife isn't a crisis at all? What if it's an invitation?

The jazz musician Charlie Haden never learned to read music. He played entirely by ear, feeling his way through compositions with an intuitive brilliance that classically trained musicians envied. When asked how he knew what notes to play, he explained, "I don't think about the notes. I listen for where the music wants to go."

Your life at forty is like that—less about following a predetermined score and more about developing the sensitivity to hear where your particular music wants to go next.

This isn't new age wishful thinking. It's neuroscience. Around midlife, our brains actually undergo subtle changes that enhance integrative thinking. We become better at seeing connections between disparate ideas, more adept at holding contradictions, more capable of wisdom that transcends binary thinking. While culture tells us we're in decline, our brains are actually evolving toward a more sophisticated intelligence—one that prioritizes meaning over achievement, depth over speed.

The novelist George Eliot published her masterpiece "Middlemarch" at age 52, after years of writing under a male pseudonym to be taken seriously. What's remarkable isn't just the late timing but the nature of the work itself. "Middlemarch" is a novel about ordinary people living ordinary lives in an ordinary town—yet it's considered one of the greatest novels ever written precisely because Eliot saw the extraordinary significance in seemingly insignificant lives. She understood that meaning isn't found in grand gestures but in the texture of daily existence, in what she called "the growing good of the world...half owing to the number who lived faithfully a hidden life."

Perhaps that's the revolution waiting for you at forty. Not a dramatic reinvention, but a quiet recognition that the life you're already living—with all its contradictions, disappointments, and unexpected joys—is enough. Not because you're settling, but because you're finally seeing.

In his research on happiness, psychologist Mihaly Csikszentmihalyi found that people report the highest levels of wellbeing not when they're pursuing happiness directly, but when they're so absorbed in meaningful activity that they lose track of themselves entirely. He called this state "flow." Flow doesn't come from finding the perfect thing to do with your life. It comes from bringing your full presence to whatever you're doing right now.

It's worth asking: When was the last time you felt fully alive? Not accomplished or praised or validated—but alive? It probably wasn't when you were checking boxes on your life plan. It was likely when you were so immersed in something that you forgot to check the time. That's not purpose finding you. That's you finding presence.

A woman named Elaine spent twenty years climbing the corporate ladder only to find herself at forty-two staring out her corner office window wondering whose life she was living. She didn't quit dramatically. She didn't have an epiphany. She simply started paying attention differently.

She noticed what made time disappear for her—cooking elaborate meals for friends, troubleshooting complex problems at work, teaching her nephew to play chess. Not one of these became her "new purpose." Collectively, they became the texture of a life she was no longer postponing until she figured it out.

Five years later, Elaine was still at the same company. Her life looked remarkably similar on paper. But she lived it entirely differently—with an attention that transformed mundane moments into meaningful ones. Her crisis wasn't resolved by finding a new thing to do with her life. It was resolved by showing up differently for the life she already had.

Too often, we mistake purpose for product—something we create and present to the world for validation. But what if purpose is more like a garden? Not something you build once and complete, but something you tend daily, something cyclical and seasonal, something that feeds you precisely because you keep showing up for it.

This insight doesn't sell many self-help books. It doesn't fuel the personal growth industry. It doesn't go viral on social media. It's too simple, too obvious, too lacking in five-step plans and downloadable worksheets. But it might be the truest thing about midlife: The way forward isn't finding the answer. It's learning to live richly inside the questions.

Our culture valorizes certainty. We celebrate the visionaries, the ones who always knew what they wanted, who pursued singular goals with unwavering focus. We sideline the meandering journeys, the multiple careers, the quiet evolutions. But what if the winding path isn't the consolation prize? What if it's the point?

Psychologist Barry Schwartz has written extensively about what he calls "the paradox of choice"—the counterintuitive finding that more options often make us less happy, not more. We become paralyzed by possibilities, haunted by the ghosts of paths not taken. When you're forty and unsure, the world can feel like an overwhelming menu of paths you should have chosen earlier.

But Schwartz's research reveals something remarkable: The happiest people aren't those who make the objectively "best" choices. They're those who fully commit to their choices once made, who don't perpetually wonder about the road not taken. The satisfaction comes not from choosing perfectly but from embracing wholeheartedly.

This is the hidden doorway at midlife. You don't need to find the perfect path forward. You need to walk fully on the path you're already on, even as it curves and changes.

There's a profound difference between asking "What should I do with my life?" and asking "How can I be more fully alive in this one?" The first question assumes life is something separate from you, a project to be managed. The second recognizes that you are your life—not its architect but its embodiment.

I'm reminded of the poet Mary Oliver's instructions for living: "Pay attention. Be astonished. Tell about it." Notice she doesn't say "Find your purpose. Execute your plan.

Achieve your goals." Her instructions are about presence, not performance. About wonder, not work. About expression, not impression.

This might be the most subversive truth of all: You don't need to do anything special with your life to justify having lived it. Your existence isn't a business proposal requiring an ROI. You aren't behind on some cosmic deadline. You haven't missed boarding for the last train to significance.

The man who never figured it all out is thriving not because he finally found the answer, but because he made peace with the questions. He stopped treating his uncertainty as evidence of failure and started treating it as an invitation to presence. He stopped trying to find what to do with his life and started noticing he was already living it—in conversations with friends, in moments of unexpected beauty, in small kindnesses exchanged with strangers, in work that absorbed him without defining him.

What if that's the real secret? What if the point isn't to find what to do with your life—it's to live it? To feel the sun on your face without needing to justify the sensation. To love without guarantees. To work, not because it validates your existence, but because there's satisfaction in contribution. To laugh without documenting it. To cry without apologizing for it.

Maybe when you stop trying to find what to do with your life, you create space for your life to find you—in all its messy, unplanned, beautiful ordinariness. Maybe that's not settling. Maybe that's freedom.

This isn't just philosophical musing. It's practical liberation. When you release yourself from the tyranny of having to figure it all out, you open yourself to experiences you might otherwise filter out, connections you might otherwise dismiss, possibilities you might otherwise overlook because they don't fit your predetermined narrative of what should come next.

At forty, you're old enough to know that plans rarely unfold as expected. You're wise enough to recognize that control is largely an illusion. What if you embraced that wisdom instead of fighting it? What if uncertainty became not your enemy but your ally?

The point isn't finding what to do with your life. The point is living it—fully awake, deeply connected, undefended against its mysteries. The point is showing up for what's actually happening, not what you think should be happening.

You haven't failed because you haven't figured it out. You've simply arrived at the threshold where the most important questions don't have answers. They have invitations. And the invitation is always the same: Wake up. Be here. Stay curious. This is your life. It's happening right now. Don't miss it while you're busy planning it.

Conclusion: This Is Not the End of Something. It's a Middle Worth Loving.

We've come to the end of these essays, but really, we're still in the middle of the conversation. Just as you're in the middle of your story. Not at the beginning, with its sweet naivety and boundless possibility. Not at the end, with its quiet reconciliations and backward glances. But gloriously, complicatedly in the middle—where the action is.

The middle gets a bad reputation. In stories, we call it "the muddle in the middle" where plots often sag. In lives, we call it "midlife" and attach the word "crisis." We're conditioned to believe that beginnings sparkle with promise, endings glow with resolution, but middles? Middles are to be endured, pushed through, survived.

What if we've misunderstood the entire concept?

The middle is where characters develop depth. It's where plots thicken and intertwine. It's where the easy answers of youth meet the complexities of experience. The middle is not something to escape—it's the richest terrain of existence.

At forty-something, you stand at a vantage point that offers both perspective and possibility. You can look back with enough distance to see patterns. You can look forward with enough runway to create meaningful change. This position—this middle—is not a consolation prize for missing your youth. It's the main event.

Throughout these essays, we've challenged the conventional wisdom about what constitutes a successful, well-lived life. We've questioned the tyranny of timelines, the conflation of identity with occupation, the fetishization of certainty. We've pushed back against the subtle cultural suggestion that by midlife, the die should already be cast, the path already set.

The actor Alan Rickman was a professional graphic designer until age 42, when he landed his first major film role. In interviews years later, he spoke about how his "late" entry into serious acting gave him an advantage—a lifetime of observation, a developed sense of self, and freedom from the desperate ambition that often plagues younger actors. "I was in the luxurious position of having a growth that was not visible to the public or on YouTube," he once said. His path made no sense to many observers, but as we've discovered, the most meaningful paths rarely conform to external logic.

I've sat with countless people at midlife crossroads, people whose external markers of success—titles, salaries, possessions—masked a growing sense of disconnect. Their questions often follow a similar pattern: "Is this all there is?" or "What's wrong with me that I can't just be satisfied?" or "Am I too old to start something new?"

Behind each question lies the same core fear: that they've somehow missed the boat, that there was a right way to do life and they've failed to find it, that it's too late now to correct course.

This fear is not irrational. We live in a culture obsessed with prodigies, "30 under 30" lists, and narratives about knowing your passion from childhood. We're bombarded with messaging that success comes from early specialization and straight-line career trajectories. We're fed the myth that fulfillment is found through arriving at some fixed destination—the right job, the right relationship, the right life.

But what if all of that is wrong?

The research on adult development tells a different story. Psychologist Daniel Levinson's landmark studies on adult life phases propose that the "midlife transition" (roughly 40-45) represents not a crisis but a natural developmental stage—a time when adults typically reassess their lives and make significant adjustments. Far from being abnormal, this questioning is part of healthy psychological development.

Developmental psychologist Erik Erikson framed middle adulthood as centered around the crisis of "generativity versus stagnation"—a time when we either find ways to contribute to the world beyond ourselves or become self-absorbed and stagnant. This framing suggests that midlife questioning isn't selfish navel-gazing; it's a crucial engagement with how you'll direct your energy for the second half of life.

The playwright Tom Stoppard didn't write his masterpiece "Arcadia" until he was in his fifties. When asked why his later plays seemed to have more emotional depth than his earlier, more technically brilliant work, he replied simply: "I had to live more." There's wisdom in that. Some creative contributions can only emerge after decades of living—not because of technical skill development, but because of the emotional and spiritual maturation that only time allows.

So here you are, in the middle. Not lost. Not late. Just alive at a particular moment in your unfolding story.

The antidote to midlife malaise isn't a five-year plan or a radical reinvention (though either might be part of your path). The antidote is presence—the willingness to show up fully for your life as it exists right now, while remaining open to how it might evolve. To notice what actually engages you, not what's supposed to. To follow your curiosity even when it leads to places that make no sense on paper.

Freedom comes not from having all the answers, but from asking better questions. Questions like:

What would I do if I weren't afraid of looking foolish? What activities make me lose track of time? If salary and status were removed from the equation, what work would still matter to me? What have I been curious about but never allowed myself to explore? Where do I feel most like myself?

These questions don't demand immediate answers. They're invitations to inquiry, prompts for ongoing conversation with yourself. They acknowledge that knowing what to do with your life isn't a single decision but a series of choices made daily, weekly, yearly—choices that can and should evolve as you do.

In his quietly revolutionary book "Designing Your Life," Stanford professor Bill Burnett makes a compelling case that the best way forward when you're stuck isn't more analysis; it's action. Small experiments. Prototype experiences. Conversations with people doing interesting things. The path clarifies through movement, not contemplation alone.

Movement doesn't require dramatic gestures. You don't need to quit your job tomorrow, sell your possessions, or announce to the world that you're "finding yourself." Those grand declarations often come from the same place as the rigid certainty you're trying to escape—the belief that identity is fixed, that decisions are permanent, that life must follow a coherent narrative.

What if, instead, you simply allowed yourself to become interested in things? To follow threads of curiosity without needing to justify them? To expand rather than replace your existing life?

A client once described her midlife questioning this way: "I kept looking for the neon sign that would tell me exactly what to do next. Then I realized there is no sign. There's just paying attention to what actually engages me, not what I think should engage me."

For her, this meant noticing how alive she felt volunteering with a local theater group—something she'd dismissed as "just a hobby" for years. It wasn't about turning the hobby into a career. It was about honoring that this activity brought her alive in ways her prestigious consulting job never had, and gradually adjusting her life to include more of what energized her.

Small shifts. Paying attention. Moving toward energy rather than away from discomfort.

The psychologist Barry Schwartz has extensively studied how more choice often leads to less satisfaction—what he calls "the paradox of choice." When presented with too many options, we become paralyzed, then dissatisfied with whatever we eventually choose. His research suggests that the relentless pursuit of the "best" option (what he calls "maximizing") leads to poorer outcomes than accepting "good enough" ("satisficing").

Applied to midlife questioning, this research offers liberating possibilities. What if there isn't one perfect answer to what you should do with your life? What if there are many potentially satisfying paths? What if the goal isn't to find the optimal answer but to choose a direction that's aligned with your values and interests, then commit to it wholeheartedly?

This perspective doesn't diminish the importance of the question. It expands the range of acceptable answers.

I think of a former colleague—a successful attorney who, at 46, realized she'd been asking herself the wrong question.

Instead of "What should I do with my life?" she started asking, "Who do I want to spend it with?" This subtle shift led her not to change careers but to restructure her existing work to allow more time with the people who mattered most to her. Her title remained the same, but her life changed profoundly.

This is the paradoxical freedom of the middle: you know enough to recognize what matters, and you likely have enough resources and agency to act on that knowledge. You may have more constraints than you did at twenty—financial obligations, family responsibilities, community commitments—but you also have more clarity, more skills, more perspective on what actually brings fulfillment.

Those constraints aren't obstacles to freedom; they're the context within which meaningful freedom operates. As the poet David Whyte observes, "Freedom is not the absence of limitation and constraint but the discovery of possibility within a chosen limitation." The limits define the form; the form enables the expression.

So here's my final provocation: What if you're not stuck at all? What if you're actually, finally free?

Free from the desperate striving to prove yourself that characterized your twenties and thirties. Free from measuring your worth against external metrics of success. Free from the illusion that certainty exists or that anyone else has found it. Free to create a life based not on what you're supposed to want, but on what actually engages your heart and mind.

This freedom isn't granted by external circumstances. It comes from the willingness to question everything you've been told about what makes a good life, combined with the courage to act on what you discover.

The novelist George Eliot wrote, "It's never too late to be what you might have been." I'd amend that slightly: It's never too late to become who you already are beneath the layers of shoulds and supposed-tos. The invitation of midlife isn't to become someone new, but to more fully inhabit the person you've always been—with all your contradictions, complexities, and potential still waiting to unfold.

Stop looking for a label and start noticing your life. The moments that light you up. The people who make you feel most yourself. The activities that engage your full attention. These aren't trivial data points; they're breadcrumbs leading you home to yourself.

You didn't miss the train. You're not behind schedule. You're not failing some cosmic test of adulthood.

You're building your own tracks, on your own timeline, toward a destination that might not yet be clear. And that's not just okay—it's the point of the whole journey.

The middle isn't something to get through. It's something to get into. To inhabit fully. To recognize as the heart of the story—your story—still unfolding, still full of possibility, still yours to write.

A Tiny Favor That Would Mean the World to Me

If you enjoyed this book and found it helpful, I would be truly grateful if you could take a moment to leave a review on Amazon.

It doesn't have to be long — even a few words make a huge difference.

Reviews help more people discover the book, and they let me know that the ideas inside have made an impact.

It would absolutely make my day to hear that something in these pages helped you, challenged you, or gave you a new way of seeing the world.

Thank you so much for reading — and for being part of this journey.

JM

My Other Books

How To Become Smarter: 14 Unconventional Lessons To Elevate Your Life Choices, Career and Confidence

Available on Amazon: ebook, audiobook, paperback

How To Be Respected: 14 Unconventional Lessons on How You Earn Respect—and Keep It

Available on Amazon: ebook, audiobook, paperback

What to Do With Your Life When You Have Indecision: 14 Unconventional Lessons

Available on Amazon: ebook, audiobook, paperback

Acknowledgments

After publishing my previous book, What to Do with Your Life, many readers who enjoyed it reached out to seek guidance on managing life indecision in their late thirties and beyond, sharing their stories and their fears. This book would not exist without them. Thank you.

To Melissa, Paul and JD my incredibly talented editors. Working with you daily is not only making me a better writer. It's making me a better human being.

To my family, who (I know I keep & keep saying this) never once stopped believing in me, even when I had stopped believing in myself - and this happened more times than I wish it did - thank you for your positivity and patience.

And to all the thinkers, writers, athletes, artists, and rebels —known and unknown—whose unconventional wisdom keep lighting and enlighten the path: this book is a thank-you letter in essay form.

About Jake

Jake Morimoto has been writing quietly for years. A lifelong notetaker and lover of contrarian ideas, he finally decided to share his work with the world. *Think Against* is his publishing debut—a sharp, distilled manifesto for those who think sideways. He lives simply, writes daily, and prefers questions to answers.

Bibliography

INTRODUCTION

Carstensen, L. L. (2006). The influence of a sense of time on human development. *Science*, 312(5782), 1913-1915.

DuVernay, A. (2015). *Interview with The Hollywood Reporter*, March 14, 2015.

Eliot, G. (1871). *Middlemarch: A Study of Provincial Life.*

Epstein, D. (2019). *Range: Why Generalists Triumph in a Specialized World.* Riverhead Books.

Jung, C. G. (1933). *Modern Man in Search of a Soul.* Harcourt, Brace & World.

Linehan, M. M. (2015). *DBT Skills Training Manual.* Guilford Publications.

Munger, C. T. (1995). *Speech at USC Business School.*

CHAPTER 1

Foster Wallace, D. (2005). *This is Water: Some Thoughts, Delivered on a Significant Occasion, about Living a Compassionate Life.*

Gilbert, D., & Quoidbach, J. (2013). The end of history illusion. Science, 339(6115), 96-98.

Gilligan, C. (1993). In a Different Voice: Psychological Theory and Women's Development.

Hollis, J. (2005). Finding Meaning in the Second Half of Life: How to Finally, Really Grow Up.

Ibarra, H. (2003). Working Identity: Unconventional Strategies for Reinventing Your Career.

Urschel, J. (2017, July 27). Why I'm retiring from the NFL at age 26. Sports Illustrated.

CHAPTER 2

Eliot, G. (1871). Middlemarch: A Study of Provincial Life.

Galenson, D. W. (2007). Old Masters and Young Geniuses: The Two Life Cycles of Artistic Creativity. Princeton University Press.

Gladwell, M. (2008). Late Bloomers: Why do we equate genius with precocity? The New Yorker, October 20, 2008.

Jones, B. F. (2010). Age and Great Invention. The Review of Economics and Statistics, 92(1), 1-14.

Rogers, C. (1961). On Becoming a Person: A Therapist's View of Psychotherapy. Houghton Mifflin.

Simonton, D. K. (1991). Career Landmarks in Science: Individual Differences and Interdisciplinary Contrasts. Developmental Psychology, 27(1), 119-130.

Warner, K., & Silver, M. (2000). All Things Possible: My Story of Faith, Football, and the First Miracle Season. HarperCollins.

CHAPTER 3

Bateson, M. C. (1990). Composing a Life. Plume.

Jaques, E. (1965). Death and the mid-life crisis. International Journal of Psychoanalysis, 46, 502-514.

Maslow, A. H. (1968). Toward a Psychology of Being. Van Nostrand Reinhold Company.

Robinson, O., & Stell, A. J. (2015). Later-life crisis: Towards a holistic model. Journal of Adult Development, 22(1), 38-49.

Ryff, C. D., & Singer, B. H. (2008). Know thyself and become what you are: A eudaimonic approach to psychological well-being. Journal of Happiness Studies, 9(1), 13-39.

Stokes, M. (2012). Marion Stokes Television News Archive. Internet Archive.

Strenger, C., & Ruttenberg, A. (2008). The existential necessity of midlife change. Harvard Business Review, 86(2), 82-90.

CHAPTER 4

Clear, J. (2018). *Atomic Habits: An Easy & Proven Way to Build Good Habits & Break Bad Ones*. Avery.

Epstein, D. (2019). *Range: Why Generalists Triumph in a Specialized World*. Riverhead Books.

Ferriss, T. (2007). *The 4-Hour Workweek: Escape 9-5, Live Anywhere, and Join the New Rich*. Crown Publishing Group.

Godin, S. (2007). *The Dip: A Little Book That Teaches You When to Quit (and When to Stick)*. Portfolio.

Honeyman, G. (2017). *Eleanor Oliphant Is Completely Fine*. HarperCollins.

Ibarra, H. (2004). *Working Identity: Unconventional Strategies for Reinventing Your Career*. Harvard Business Review Press.

Ries, E. (2011). *The Lean Startup: How Today's Entrepreneurs Use Continuous Innovation to Create Radically Successful Businesses*. Crown Business.

CHAPTER 5

Bateson, M. C. (1990). *Composing a Life*. Plume.

Epley, N. & Schroeder, J. (2014). Mistakenly seeking solitude. *Journal of Experimental Psychology: General*, 143(5), 1980-1999.

Frankl, V. E. (1959). *Man's Search for Meaning*. Beacon Press.

Gilbert, D. (2006). *Stumbling on Happiness*. Knopf.

Little, B. R. (2014). *Me, Myself, and Us: The Science of Personality and the Art of Well-Being*. PublicAffairs.

Steger, M. F., Oishi, S., & Kashdan, T. B. (2009). Meaning in life across the life span: Levels and correlates of meaning in life from emerging adulthood to older adulthood. *The Journal of Positive Psychology*, 4(1), 43-52.

Wrzesniewski, A., & Dutton, J. E. (2001). Crafting a job: Revisioning employees as active crafters of their work. *Academy of Management Review*, 26(2), 179-201.

CHAPTER 6

Arkes, H. R., & Blumer, C. (1985). The psychology of sunk cost. *Organizational Behavior and Human Decision Processes*, 35(1), 124-140.

Duke, A. (2018). *Thinking in Bets: Making Smarter Decisions When You Don't Have All the Facts*. Portfolio.

Godin, S. (2007). *The Dip: A Little Book That Teaches You When to Quit (and When to Stick)*. Portfolio.

Kahneman, D. (2011). *Thinking, Fast and Slow*. Farrar, Straus and Giroux.

Kegan, R., & Lahey, L. L. (2009). *Immunity to Change: How to Overcome It and Unlock the Potential in Yourself and Your Organization*. Harvard Business Press.

Shah, J. Y., Friedman, R., & Kruglanski, A. W. (2002). Forgetting all else: On the antecedents and consequences of goal shielding. *Journal of Personality and Social Psychology*, 83(6), 1261-1280.

CHAPTER 7

Brighton, M. (1986). "Breaking the Vessel: Reflections on Artistic Identity." Vermont Arts Quarterly, 12(3), 45-52.

Carstensen, L. L. (2006). "The influence of a sense of time on human development." Science, 312(5782), 1913-1915.

Frankl, V. E. (1959). Man's Search for Meaning. Beacon Press.

Fromm, E. (1955). The Sane Society. Rinehart & Company.

Hollis, J. (2005). Finding Meaning in the Second Half of Life. Gotham Books.

Lightman, A. (2005). A Sense of the Mysterious: Science and the Human Spirit. Pantheon Books.

Vaillant, G. E. (2012). Triumphs of Experience: The Men of the Harvard Grant Study. Harvard University Press.

Williams, W. C. (1951). The Autobiography of William Carlos Williams. Random House.

Wrzesniewski, A. (2003). "Jobs, careers, and callings: People's relations to their work." Journal of Research in Personality, 31, 21-33.

CHAPTER 8

Csikszentmihalyi, M. (1990). Flow: The Psychology of Optimal Experience. Harper & Row.

Fetell Lee, I. (2018). Joyful: The Surprising Power of Ordinary Things to Create Extraordinary Happiness. Little, Brown Spark.

Maffetone, P. (2010). The Big Book of Endurance Training and Racing. Skyhorse Publishing.

Mayo, E. (1949). The Social Problems of an Industrial Civilization. Routledge.

Microsoft Japan. (2019). "Work-Life Choice Challenge 2019 Summer" Press Release.

NASA Johnson Space Center. (1995). "Fatigue and Performance in the Workplace: Current Knowledge and Future Directions." Technical Report.

Pang, A.S. (2016). Rest: Why You Get More Done When You Work Less. Basic Books.

Spurling, H. (2005). Matisse the Master: A Life of Henri Matisse, Volume 2. Knopf.

Zijlstra, F. R. H., & Sonnentag, S. (2006). "After work is done: Psychological perspectives on recovery from work." European Journal of Work and Organizational Psychology, 15(2), 129-138.

CHAPTER 9

Brown, S. (2009). Play: How it Shapes the Brain, Opens the Imagination, and Invigorates the Soul. Avery.

California Institute of Creativity. (2018). "Amateur Pursuits and Professional Performance: Correlations and Causalities." Journal of Creative Behavior, 52(4), 267-281.

Knapp, C. (2003). "Making the Most of the In-Between." The Missouri Review, 26(1), 95-110.

Langer, E. (2014). Mindfulness: 25th Anniversary Edition. Da Capo Lifelong Books.

Oldenburg, R. (1999). The Great Good Place: Cafes, Coffee Shops, Bookstores, Bars, Hair Salons, and Other Hangouts at the Heart of a Community. Da Capo Press.

Suits, B. (1978). The Grasshopper: Games, Life and Utopia. University of Toronto Press.

University of Michigan Center for Social Research. (2019). "Community Connection Through Amateur Activities." Journal of Leisure Research, 41(3), 328-342.

CHAPTER 10

Boo, Katherine. Behind the Beautiful Forevers: Life, Death, and Hope in a Mumbai Undercity. Random House, 2012.

Fenn, Lisa. Carry On: A Story of Resilience, Redemption, and an Unlikely Family. Harper, 2016.

Lyubomirsky, Sonja and Kristin Layous. "How Do Simple Positive Activities Increase Well-Being?" Current Directions in Psychological Science, 2013.

Munger, Charlie. Poor Charlie's Almanack: The Wit and Wisdom of Charles T. Munger. Donning Company Publishers, 2005.

Seligman, Martin. Flourish: A Visionary New Understanding of Happiness and Well-being. Free Press, 2011.

Solnit, Rebecca. The Faraway Nearby. Viking, 2013.

CHAPTER 11

Bourdain, Anthony. Kitchen Confidential: Adventures in the Culinary Underbelly. Bloomsbury Publishing, 2000.

Eliot, George. Middlemarch. William Blackwood and Sons, 1871-72.

Kierkegaard, Søren. Fear and Trembling. Penguin Classics, 1985 (originally published 1843).

McAdams, Dan P. The Stories We Live By: Personal Myths and the Making of the Self. Guilford Press, 1993.

Nussbaum, Martha C. Cultivating Humanity: A Classical Defense of Reform in Liberal Education. Harvard University Press, 1997.

Oliver, Mary. "The Summer Day" in New and Selected Poems. Beacon Press, 1992.

Sheldon, Kennon M. and Andrew J. Elliot. "Goal striving, need satisfaction, and longitudinal well-being: The self-concordance model." Journal of Personality and Social Psychology, 1999.

CHAPTER 12

Frankl, Viktor E. Man's Search for Meaning: An Introduction to Logotherapy. Beacon Press, 1959.

Kashdan, Todd B. and Jonathan Rottenberg. "Psychological flexibility as a fundamental aspect of health." Clinical Psychology Review, vol. 30, no. 7, 2010, pp. 865-878.

Leakey, Mary D. Disclosing the Past: An Autobiography. Doubleday, 1984.

Pessoa, Fernando. The Book of Disquiet. Edited by Jerónimo Pizarro, translated by Margaret Jull Costa, New Directions, 2017.

Rodin, Auguste. Art: Conversations with Paul Gsell. University of California Press, 1984.

Santmyer, Helen Hooven. "...And Ladies of the Club." Ohio State University Press, 1982.

CHAPTER 13

Dweck, Carol S. *Mindset: The New Psychology of Success.* Random House, 2006.

Kegan, Robert. *In Over Our Heads: The Mental Demands of Modern Life.* Harvard University Press, 1994.

Morrison, Toni. *The Source of Self-Regard: Selected Essays, Speeches, and Meditations.* Knopf, 2019.

Nyad, Diana. *Find a Way: The Inspiring Story of One Woman's Pursuit of a Lifelong Dream.* Knopf, 2015.

Schwartz, Tony and Catherine McCarthy. "Manage Your Energy, Not Your Time." Harvard Business Review, October 2007.

CHAPTER 14

Bateson, M. C. (1990). *Composing a Life.* Plume.

Bellah, R. N., Madsen, R., Sullivan, W. M., Swidler, A., & Tipton, S. M. (1985). *Habits of the Heart: Individualism and Commitment in American Life.* University of California Press.

Csikszentmihalyi, M. (1990). *Flow: The Psychology of Optimal Experience.* Harper & Row.

Eliot, G. (1871). *Middlemarch.* William Blackwood & Sons.

Feynman, R. P. (1985). *"Surely You're Joking, Mr. Feynman!": Adventures of a Curious Character.* W. W. Norton & Company.

Heidegger, M. (1962). *Being and Time.* Harper & Row.

Oliver, M. (2008). *Red Bird: Poems*. Beacon Press.

Schwartz, B. (2004). *The Paradox of Choice: Why More Is Less*. Ecco.

CONCLUSION

Burnett, B., & Evans, D. (2016). *Designing Your Life: How to Build a Well-Lived, Joyful Life*. Knopf.

Erikson, E. H. (1959). *Identity and the Life Cycle*. W. W. Norton & Company.

Levinson, D. J. (1978). *The Seasons of a Man's Life*. Ballantine Books.

Rickman, A. (2015). *Interview with The Guardian*, April 15, 2015.

Schwartz, B. (2004). *The Paradox of Choice: Why More Is Less*. Harper Perennial.

Stoppard, T. (2001). *Interview with The Paris Review*, Fall 2001.

Whyte, D. (2002). *Clear Mind, Wild Heart* (Audio Learning Course). Sounds True.

www.ingramcontent.com/pod-product-compliance
Lightning Source LLC
Chambersburg PA
CBHW020930090426
42736CB00010B/1092